THE
BATTLE OVER
HOMEWORK

Faye Norflus Cooper, for the wonderful things
she passed on to her grandchildren,
through me.

Second Edition

THE
BATTLE OVER
HOMEWORK

HARRIS COOPER

Common Ground for
Administrators, Teachers, and Parents

CORWIN PRESS, INC.
A Sage Publications Company
Thousand Oaks, California

For information:

Corwin Press, Inc.
A Sage Publications Company
2455 Teller Road
Thousand Oaks, California 91320
E-mail: order@corwinpress.com

Sage Publications Ltd.
6 Bonhill Street
London EC2A 4PU
United Kingdom

Sage Publications India Pvt. Ltd.
M-32 Market
Greater Kailash I
New Delhi 110 048 India

Printed in the United States of America

Library of Congress Cataloging-in-Publication Data

Cooper, Harris M.
  The battle over homework: Common ground for administrators, teachers, and parents / by Harris Cooper.— 2nd ed.
    p. cm.
  Includes bibliographical references
  ISBN 0-7619-7820-8 (cloth) — ISBN 0-7619-7821-6 (paper)
  1. Homework. I. Title.
LB1048 .C655 2001
371.3′028′1—dc21   00-012348

This book is printed on acid-free paper.

01 02 03 04 05 06 07 7 6 5 4 3 2 1

Acquiring Editor:	Rachel Livsey
Corwin Editorial Assistant:	Phyllis Cappello
Production Editor:	Diane S. Foster
Editorial Assistant:	Cindy Bear
Typesetter/Designer:	Denyse Dunn
Cover Designer:	Michael Dubowe

Contents

Preface   ix

About the Author   xiv

1. Finding the Common Ground   1
The American Public's Attitudes Toward Homework   1
A Definition of Homework   3
   What Are Some Ways That Homework
    Assignments Can Differ From One Another?   3
The Effects of Homework   6
   What Are the Suggested Positive Effects of Homework? 6
   What Are the Suggested Negative Effects of Homework? 8
Factors Affecting the Utility of Homework   10

2. Does Homework Work?   13
Homework Versus No Homework   13
   Is Homework Better Than No Homework at All?   14
   Do Homework Effects Vary With Grade Level?   14
   What About Other Student Differences?   14
   Is Subject Matter Important?   15
   Does Homework Affect All Achievement
    Measures Equally?   15
   What About the Frequency and Length of Assignments?   16
   Does Homework Affect Students' Attitudes?   16
Homework Versus In-School Supervised Study   16
   Is Homework Better Than In-School Study?   17
   Does Grade Level Influence the Effects of the
    Two Strategies?   17
   What About Subject Matter?   18

Is the Type of Achievement Measure Important? 18
What About Nonacademic Outcomes? 18
Are After-School Homework Programs Effective? 19
Grade Level, Learning Disabilities, and the Value of
  Homework 19
Why Is the Relation Between Homework and
  Achievement So Weak for Young Children? 20
Should Children With Learning Disabilities
  Be Assigned Homework? 20
Understanding the Size of Homework's Effect 22
Summary 23

3. **Time Spent on Homework Assignments** 24
The Simple Relation Between Homework Time and
  Academic Outcomes 25
Is Time Spent on Homework Related to Achievement
  or Attitudes? 26
Does Grade Level Have an Effect? 26
Does the Frequency or Length of Assignments Matter? 28
Is Subject Matter Important? 28
What About Achievement Versus Attitudes? 29
Do Student Differences Matter? 29
Does Time Spent on Homework Cause Achievement
  Differences? 30
The Curvilinear Relation Between Homework Time
  and Achievement 31
Is There an Optimum Amount of Homework? 31
What About Causality? 32
Summary 33

4. **The Homework Assignment** 35
Content of Assignments 35
Is the Timing of Homework and Its Related Work
  in Class Important? 35
Should Teachers Individualize Assignments Within
  a Class? 37
Should Homework Be Compulsory or Voluntary? 38

Teacher Feedback and Incentives   39
   Are Comments and Grading Important to the
     Utility of Homework?   39
   What About Providing Incentives?   40
Summary   40

5. **Home and Community Influences on Homework**   41
Competitors for Student Time   41
   Does Watching Television Affect Achievement?   42
   Do High School Students Who Have After-School Jobs
     Perform Well in School?   42
   What About Extracurricular and Other Structured
     Group Activities?   43
   Summary   43
The Home Environment and Parent Involvement   44
   What Can Happen When Parents Become Involved
     in Homework?   44
   Is Parent Involvement Associated With a Student's
     Academic Achievement?   45
   Why Is the Research Inconclusive?   46
   What Are Some Ways That Parents Can Become
     Involved in Homework?   46
   Are Some Types of Parent Involvement More
     Beneficial Than Others?   47
   Does Grade Level Make a Difference?   47
   What About the Parents' Role in Creating a Good
     Environment for Doing Homework?   48
   Do Homework Hotlines and Web Sites Help?   48
Summary   49

6. **Homework Policies for School Districts,**
   Schools, and Classrooms   50
Current Policies of School Districts   50
The Department of Education's *What Works*   52
The PTA and the NEA   54
Kappa Delta Pi   58
Other Sources of Policy Guidelines   63

Policy Statements Based on the Present Review   64
    What Should Be Contained in District Homework
      Policies?   64
    What Should Be Contained in School Policies?   67
    What Should Be Contained in Classroom Policies?   67
  Summary   68

7. **Quick Tips for Parents and Students**   72
  The PTA and the NEA   72
  The Office of Educational Research and Improvement
    (OERI)   74
  Conclusion   77

References   79

Preface

How much time should children spend doing homework? Should elementary school children do any homework at all? Do both high and low achievers benefit from homework? What role should parents play in the homework process?

Homework is a source of complaint and friction between home and school more often than any other teaching activity. Parents protest that assignments are too long or too short, too hard or too easy, too ambiguous. Teachers complain about a lack of training, a lack of time to prepare effective assignments, and a lack of support from parents and administrators. Students gripe about the time homework takes from their leisure activities, if they understand the value of the exercise at all.

These complaints are not surprising, considering that homework assignments are influenced by more factors than any other instructional strategy. Teachers can structure and monitor homework in a multitude of ways. Student differences play a major role because homework allows students considerable discretion about whether, when, and how to complete assignments. The home environment influences the process by creating an atmosphere that fosters or inhibits study. Finally, the broader community plays a role by providing other leisure activities that compete for the student's time.

I have written this book to help everyone involved in the process make sound decisions about homework. My objective is to provide readers with the terms, definitions, and research evidence needed to hold conversations about homework in a constructive manner. Also, I hope to help readers set effective homework policies, rules, or guidelines, be they for a school district, a school, a classroom, or a family.

The book speaks to all the parties in the homework process—administrators, teachers, parents, and students. A key to ending the battle over homework is communication. It is critically important for all parties to know what others are doing and why. To help communication, much of the material in the book is presented in a question-and-answer format. I did this to make it easy for readers to find answers to the questions that concern them most.

Administrators can use this book not only to help develop policies but also to assist in explaining to teachers and parents the rationale behind the homework guidelines they set. Likewise, teachers can use the book to inform their classroom practices and to assist in justifying those practices to parents and students. Parents will find some practical advice regarding how to help their children with homework and to find insight into why certain practices are followed by schools and teachers. But most important, I hope the book is used by administrators, teachers, and parents together to make their discussions about homework a positive experience and to help resolve disagreements.

The book addresses homework issues at both the elementary and secondary levels. Differences in the value of homework at different grade levels, we shall see, are among homework's most interesting and revealing aspects.

The book is divided into seven chapters. Chapter 1 contains (a) a general definition of homework; (b) the important distinctions in homework assignments; (c) a list of the possible effects of homework, both positive and negative; and (d) a model of the homework process. Also, I provide a historical framework for understanding the issues and debates about homework. Chapter 2 summarizes research on whether homework is generally effective as well as on whether it is more effective for some grade levels, subjects, and types of students than for others. Chapter 3 looks at research on how much homework is best for students at different grades. Chapter 4 examines studies of variations in homework assignments that can influence their effects on achievement. Particular attention is paid to the structure of assignments, the need to be responsive to student individual differences, and the value of classroom follow-up, such as grading and feedback. Chapter 5 looks at how the community and family fit into the homework process. It offers parents some suggestions, based on research, about when and how to get involved in their students' homework. Chapter 6, written with school administrators and teachers first in mind, reviews some of the policy recommendations offered by government and private education agencies. I integrate these recommendations into a set of homework policy guidelines for school districts, schools, and classrooms. Finally, in Chapter 7, I offer quick tips for parents and students that are meant to help them use homework in an efficient and effective way.

My involvement with homework began in 1986. In that year, I received a grant from the National Science Foundation to gather, summarize, and integrate the research on the effects of homework. The role of research in forming the homework attitudes and practices of teachers, parents, and policymakers has been minimal. This is because the influences on homework are complex—no simple, general finding proving or disproving its utility is possible. However, research is plentiful enough that a few studies can be found to promote whatever position is desired while the contradictory evidence is ignored. Thus advocates for or against homework often cite isolated studies either to support or refute its value.

I had no strong predisposition favoring or opposing homework before I began. I did have a 2-year-old son at the time (with a daughter to follow shortly), so homework was about to become an issue in my family. In addition, I had much experience with rigorous techniques for summarizing research literatures (Cooper, 1998; Cooper & Hedges, 1994). Because I believe firmly that research, when exhaustively summarized and fairly treated, can positively influence educational policy and practice, I attempted to collect all research, both positive and negative, that examined the effects of homework or that compared variations in homework assignments. I then applied the most rigorous techniques to integrate the results of studies, using statistical procedures where possible.

Ultimately, my research synthesis would include nearly 120 studies, would require me to read about two times that many related pieces on homework, and would result in the first book-length assessment of homework as an instructional strategy (titled, not surprisingly, *Homework*). Since the book was published in 1989, and since the first edition of this book appeared in 1994, with support from the Department of Education, my colleagues and I have conducted an extensive survey of over 80 teachers and 700 families regarding how the homework process unfolds in their lives. Also, I have spent hundreds of hours talking with principals, teachers, and parents about homework. Those discussions, along with the literature by researchers and practicing educators and my own investigations, greatly assisted in the revision of the book and inform the contents of the pages that follow.

Too often, educators, parents, and students fall into ways of thinking that view schools and families as adversaries. Homework is a prime battleground in these conflicts. I firmly believe that the battle over homework can be avoided. Indeed, I view families as the first and principle site of learning and schools as extensions of families. When we keep these ideas in mind, homework becomes an opportunity for cooperation in learning.

ACKNOWLEDGMENTS

Thanks are extended to the National Science Foundation and the U.S. Department of Education for providing the funds I needed to carry out the research that informs this book. The opinions expressed herein are those of the author and not necessarily of the funding agencies. Thanks to my collaborators on the research, in particular Jim Lindsay and Barbara Nye. And especially, thanks to the hundreds of parents, teachers, and students who completed questionnaires and shared their ideas and experiences about homework with me. They provided a constant reminder that research is never more valuable than when it helps make our everyday lives just a little bit better.

About the Author

Harris Cooper is Professor and Chair of the Department of Psychological Science at the University of Missouri-Columbia. He received his Ph.D. in social psychology from the University of Connecticut and has been a visiting scholar at Harvard University, Stanford University, the University of Oregon, and the Russell Sage Foundation. For six years he was an elected member of the Board of Education in Columbia, Missouri, a school district serving over 16,000 students.

Dr. Cooper is widely recognized as the nation's leading expert on homework. His work has been quoted in every major print outlet in the United States, and he has appeared as a guest on *NBC Dateline*, *The Oprah Winfrey Show*, and all the major television and radio news programs.

Dr. Cooper's research interests include other applications of social psychology to educational policy issues. He has published over two dozen articles and book chapters on the formation and effects of teacher expectations. He has researched and written on the policy implications of research concerning summer school, class size, desegregation, and corporal punishment. He is the author of two books on the process of conducting research synthesis.

Dr. Cooper has been an advising editor for the *Journal of Educational Psychology*, *Elementary School Journal*, *Journal of Experimental Education*, and the *Personality and Social Psychology Bulletin*; and a guest editor of a special issue on homework for *Educational Psychologist*. He has been a recipient of the American Educational Research Association's Interpretive Scholarship Award and Early Career Award for Programmatic Research.

**CORWIN
PRESS**

The Corwin Press logo—a raven striding across an open book—represents the happy union of courage and learning. We are a professional-level publisher of books and journals for K–12 educators, and we are committed to creating and providing resources that embody these qualities. Corwin's motto is "Success for All Learners."

1

Finding the Common Ground

THE AMERICAN PUBLIC'S
ATTITUDES TOWARD HOMEWORK

Throughout the 20th century, public opinion about homework wavered between support and opposition. And almost like clockwork, the beginning of the new century has been accompanied by a controversy regarding the value of homework. Homework controversies have followed a 30-year cycle, with public outcries for more homework or less homework occurring about 15 years apart. Further complicating matters, at any moment during the past century, arguments and evidence both for and against homework simultaneously could be found in the educational literature. However, at different times the proponents and opponents of homework have alternately held sway.

Early in the past century, homework was believed to be an important means for disciplining children's minds. The mind was viewed as a muscle. Memorization—most often of material such as multiplication tables, names, and dates—not only led to knowledge acquisition but also was good mental exercise. Because memorization could be accomplished easily at home, homework was a key schooling strategy.

By the 1940s, a reaction against homework set in. Developing problem-solving ability, as opposed to learning through drill, became a central task of education. The use of homework to enhance memorization skills was called into question. Greater emphasis was placed on developing student initiative and interest in learning. Furthermore, the life-adjustment movement viewed home study as an intrusion on students' time to pursue other private, at-home activities. In the 1950 edition of *Encyclopedia of Educational Research*, H. J. Otto wrote, "Compulsory homework does not result in sufficiently improved academic accomplishments to justify retention" (p. 380).

The trend toward less homework was reversed in the late 1950s after the Russians launched the satellite Sputnik. Americans became concerned that a lack of rigor in the educational system was leaving children unprepared to face a complex technological future and to compete against our ideological adversaries. Homework was viewed as a means for accelerating the pace of knowledge acquisition.

By the mid-1960s, the cycle again reversed itself. Homework came to be seen as a symptom of too much pressure on students to achieve. Contemporary learning theories were again invoked that questioned the value of most approaches to homework. And yet again, the possible detrimental, mental-health consequences of too much homework were brought to the fore. For example, Wildman wrote in a 1968 article, "Whenever homework crowds out social experience, outdoor recreation, and creative activities, and whenever it usurps time devoted to sleep, it is not meeting the basic needs of children and adolescents" (p. 203).

In the 1980s, homework leapt back into favor. A primary stimulus behind its reemergence was the National Commission on Excellence in Education's 1983 report, *A Nation at Risk*, that cited homework as a defense against the rising tide of mediocrity in American education. The push for more homework continued into the 1990s, fueled by educators who used it to help meet increasingly rigorous, state-mandated academic standards.

As the century turned, a remarkably predictable backlash set in. Fed by beleaguered parents, newspapers and magazines were filled with articles about concern over stressed-out children. Was the increasing homework burden leading 8-year-olds to burn out? How were families, often headed by a single parent or two parents both of whom worked outside the home, to juggle work, help with homework, and have time for rest and recreation?

A DEFINITION OF HOMEWORK

Homework can be defined as tasks assigned to students by schoolteachers that are intended to be carried out during non-school hours. The word *intended* is used because students may complete homework assignments during study hall, library time, or even during subsequent classes. This definition explicitly excludes (a) in-school guided study; (b) home study courses delivered through the mail, on television, on audio- or videocassette, or over the Internet; and (c) extracurricular activities such as sports teams and clubs.

What Are Some Ways That Homework Assignments Can Differ From One Another?

Homework assignments can be classified according to their (a) amount, (b) purpose, (c) skill area, (d) degree of individualization, (e) choice for the student, (f) completion deadline, and (g) social context. Table 1.1 summarizes the distinctions in homework.

The amount of homework simply refers to the length (or how much time students spend on any particular assignment) and the frequency (or how often students receive homework assignments).

The purposes of homework assignments can be divided into instructional and noninstructional objectives. Four instructional goals are most often identified for homework. The most common purpose of homework is practice or review. Practice assignments are meant to reinforce the learning of material already presented in class and to help the student master specific skills.

Preparation assignments introduce material to be presented in future lessons. Their aim is to help students obtain the maximum benefit when the new material is covered in class by providing background information or experiences. Quite often the difference between practice and preparation homework is not in the content of the assignment but in its temporal relationship to the material being covered in class—the same material presented before class discussion is preparation, whereas after class discussion, it is practice or

Table 1.1 Distinctions in Homework Assignments

Classifications	Within Classifications
Amount	Frequency
	Length
Purpose	Instructional
	Practice
	Preparation
	Extension
	Integration
	Noninstructional
	Parent-child communication
	Fulfilling directives
	Punishment
	Community relations
Skill area used	Writing
	Reading
	Memory or retention
Degree of individualization	Geared to individual student
	Geared to groups of students
Student choice	Compulsory
	With task options
	Voluntary
Completion deadlines	Long term
	Short term
Social context	Independent
	Assisted
	Parent, sibling, other students
	Group

review. Some homework assignments can have both practice and preparation objectives by introducing new material along with the practice of old material.

The third instructional goal for homework is called extension. Extension homework involves the transfer of previously learned skills to new situations. This often requires the application of abstract principles in circumstances not covered in class. For example, students might learn about the factors that led to the French Revolution and be asked to apply them to what they know about other revolutions.

Finally, homework can serve the purpose of skill integration. Integrative homework requires the student to apply many separately learned skills and concepts to produce a single product. Examples are book reports, science projects, or creative writing.

There are other purposes of homework in addition to reinforcing or enhancing instruction. For example, homework can be used to (a) establish communication between parent and child, (b) fulfill directives from school administrators, and (c) punish students. To this list might be added the public relations objective of simply informing parents about what is going on in school.

Homework assignments rarely reflect a single purpose. Instead, most assignments have elements of several different purposes. Some of these relate to instruction, whereas others may meet the purposes of the teacher, the school administration, or even the school district.

In addition to differences in purpose, homework can call for the use of different skills. Students may be asked to read, to submit written products, or to perform drills to enhance memory or retention of material. Written products are often required to provide evidence that the assignment was completed. Drill activities involve mechanical, repetitive exercises. These might include, for example, practicing spelling words and multiplication tables, rehearsing a public speech, or memorizing vocabulary.

The degree of individualization refers to whether the teacher tailors assignments to meet the needs of each student or whether a single assignment is presented to groups of students or to the class as a whole.

The degree of choice afforded a student refers to whether the homework assignment is compulsory or voluntary. Within compulsory homework assignments, students can be given different degrees of discretion concerning which or how many parts of the assignment to complete.

Related to the degree of choice is the fact that completion deadlines for homework assignments can also vary. Some assignments are short term and meant to be completed overnight or for the next class meeting. Other assignments are long term, with students given perhaps a week or several weeks to complete the task.

Finally, homework assignments can vary according to the social context in which they are carried out. Some assignments are meant to be completed by the student independent of other people. Assisted homework explicitly calls for the involvement of another person, typically a parent but perhaps a sibling or friend. Still other assignments involve groups of students working cooperatively to produce a single product.

THE EFFECTS OF HOMEWORK

As might be expected, educators have suggested a long list of both positive and negative consequences of homework. These are listed in Table 1.2.

What Are the Suggested Positive Effects of Homework?

The positive effects of homework can be grouped into four categories: (a) immediate academic effects, (b) long-term academic effects, (c) nonacademic effects, and (d) parental-involvement effects. The immediate effects on learning are the most frequent rationales for assigning homework. Proponents of homework argue that it increases the time students spend on academic tasks. As such, the benefits of increased instructional time should accrue to students engaged in home study. Regardless of the theoretical rationale, among the suggested positive academic effects of homework are (a) better retention of factual knowledge; (b) increased understanding of material; (c) better critical thinking, concept formation, and information processing skills; and (d) enrichment of the core curriculum. Obviously, all these benefits will not accompany

Table 1.2 Positive and Negative Effects of Homework

Positive Effects

Immediate achievement and learning

> Better retention of factual knowledge
> Increased understanding
> Better critical thinking, concept formation,
>   information processing
> Curriculum enrichment

Long-term academic

> Encourage learning during leisure time
> Improved attitude toward school
> Better study habits and skills

Nonacademic

> Greater self-direction
> Greater self-discipline
> Better time organization
> More inquisitiveness
> More independent problem solving

Greater parental appreciation of and involvement in schooling

---

Negative Effects

Satiation

> Loss of interest in academic material
> Physical and emotional fatigue

Denial of access to leisure time and community activities

> Parental interference
> Pressure to complete and perform well
> Confusion of instructional techniques

Cheating

> Copying from other students
> Help beyond tutoring

Increased differences between high and low achievers

---

any single homework assignment. Instead, assignments can be tailored to promote one or more of these outcomes.

The long-term academic consequences of homework are not necessarily enhancements to achievement in particular academic domains but, rather, the establishment of general student practices that facilitate learning. Homework is expected to (a) encourage students to learn during their leisure time, (b) improve students' attitudes toward school, and (c) improve students' study habits and skills.

Homework has also been offered as a means for developing in children positive personal attributes that extend beyond academic pursuits. Because homework generally requires students to complete tasks with less supervision and under less severe time constraints than is the case in school, home study is said to promote greater self-discipline and self-direction, better time organization, more inquisitiveness, and more independent problem solving. These skills and attributes apply to the nonacademic spheres of life as well as the academic ones.

Finally, homework may have positive effects for the parents of schoolchildren. By having students bring work home for parents to see and perhaps by requesting that parents take part in the process, teachers can use homework to increase parents' appreciation of and involvement in schooling. Parental involvement may have positive effects on children as well. Students become aware of the connection between home and school. Parents can demonstrate an interest in the academic progress of their children.

What Are the Suggested Negative Effects of Homework?

Some of the negative effects attributed to homework contradict the suggested positive effects. For instance, although some have argued that homework can improve students' attitudes toward school, others counter that attitudes may be influenced negatively. They appeal to what is called a *satiation effect* as the underlying cause. That is, they argue that the potential is limited for any activity to remain rewarding. By spending increased time on school learning, children may become overexposed to academic tasks.

Thus homework may undermine good attitudes and strong achievement motivation.

Related to the *too much of a good thing* argument are the notions that homework (a) leads to general physical and emotional fatigue and (b) denies access to leisure time and community activities. Proponents of leisure activities point out that doing homework is not the only circumstance under which after-school learning takes place. Many leisure-time activities teach important academic and life skills. The key is to find the proper balance of leisure and learning.

Involving parents in the schooling process also can have negative consequences. Sometimes parents pressure students to complete homework assignments or to do them with unrealistic rigor. Parents may create confusion if they are unfamiliar with the material that is sent home for study or if their approach to learning differs from that taught in school.

In addition, parental involvement in homework can sometimes go beyond simple tutoring or assistance. We have all heard stories about science and social studies projects that display a level of detail and precision far beyond the capabilities of the student. This raises the possibility that homework might promote cheating or too much reliance on others for help with assignments. Although a lack of supervision can enhance self-direction and self-discipline, it may also lead some students to copy assignments or to receive inappropriate help from others.

Finally, some opponents of homework have argued that home study can increase differences between high- and low-achieving students, especially when the achievement difference is associated with economic differences. They suggest that high achievers from well-to-do homes will have greater parental support for home study, including more appropriate parental assistance. Also, these students are more likely to have quiet, well-lit places in which to do assignments and better resources to help them complete assignments successfully.

With a few exceptions, the positive and negative consequences of homework can occur together. For instance, homework can improve study habits at the same time that it denies access to other leisure-time activities. Some types of assignments can produce positive effects, whereas other assignments produce negative ones. In fact, in light of the host of ways homework assignments can be constructed and carried out, complex patterns of effects ought to be expected.

FACTORS AFFECTING THE UTILITY OF HOMEWORK

Table 1.3 presents a model of the homework process. The model is an attempt to organize into a single scheme all the factors that educators and parents have suggested might influence the success of a homework assignment.

Not surprisingly, the model divides the homework process into two classroom phases with a home-community phase sandwiched between. In the initial classroom phase, educators and parents suggest factors, such as teachers providing the materials needed to complete the homework (or knowing they are available in the home), that will influence whether an assignment is completed successfully. Also, teachers providing suggested approaches can be helpful, as can showing how the assignment is linked to what is going on in class. After assignments are returned to class, teachers can give different kinds of feedback, can test on homework content, and can use homework in classroom discussions. While the assignment is being carried out at home, factors that might influence its successful completion include whether other activities leave ample time, whether an appropriate setting for study is available, and whether other people can provide assistance if it is needed.

Student ability, other individual differences (such as age and economic background), and the subject matter of the assignment are viewed as the givens—as conditions that can influence the homework process. The same assignment may be more or less effective depending on the developmental level of the child and the resources available in the home. In addition, the model includes the characteristics of the assignment (described above) as potential influences on homework's effectiveness. Finally, Table 1.3 includes the potential consequences of homework as the final outcomes in the process.

Table 1.3 A Process Model of Factors Influencing the Effectiveness of Homework

Given Factors	Assignment Characteristics	Initial Classroom Factors	Home-Community Factors	Classroom Follow-Up	Outcomes Effects
Student characteristics Ability Motivation Study habits	Amount	Provision of materials	Competitors for student time	Feedback Written comments Grading Incentives	Assignment completion and performance
		Facilitators Suggested approaches			
	Purpose	Links to curriculum Other rationales	Home Environment Space Light Quiet Materials	Testing of related content	Positive effects Immediate academic Long-term academic Nonacademic parental
Subject matter	Skill area used				
Grade level	Degree of individualization		Others' involvement Parents Siblings Other students	Use in class discussion	
	Degree of student choice				Negative effects Satiation Parental Cheating Increased student differences
	Completion deadlines				
	Social context				

The model can be used to focus discussions about homework among administrators, teachers, parents, and students. It can be especially useful in identifying the factors that most influence the success of homework within a particular district, school, or classroom.

2

Does Homework Work?

One way to assess homework's effectiveness would be to compare the achievement and attitudes of students who are assigned homework with those of students who received no homework nor any other treatment meant to replace their lack of home study. Such comparisons would treat all students identically during school hours and have some but not all students complete additional academic work during nonschool hours. An alternative approach would be to compare homework with in-school supervised study. Here some students would do homework assignments at home after school and others would do the same assignments during class, during study hall, or during additional instructional time at school. It is also important in both types of comparisons that students in the two groups be as similar to one another as possible so that we know any differences are due to the way the students were treated in the study. Both types of comparisons have been used to assess the effectiveness of homework.

HOMEWORK VERSUS NO HOMEWORK

When I conducted my search of the literature in the late 1980s, I found 17 research reports that detailed the results of studies involving comparisons of homework and no-homework classrooms. The studies included over 3,300 students in 85 classrooms and 30 schools in 11 states. The studies contained a total of 48 usable comparisons.

Of the 48 comparisons, 18 used class tests or grades as the outcome measure for homework, and 30 used standardized achievement tests. Twenty-five comparisons involved achievement in
mathematics, 13 looked at reading and English, and 10 involved
science and social studies. The duration of the homework treatments
varied considerably from study to study. The length of studies
ranged from 2 to 30 weeks, averaging between 9 and 10 weeks.
The studies conducted since my literature review have been
roughly similar in design and result.

Is Homework Better Than
No Homework at All?

Yes. About 70% of comparisons indicate a positive effect for
homework. More precisely, the average student doing homework
in these studies had a higher achievement score than 55% of students
not doing homework. However, there were several important
qualifiers to this general conclusion.

Do Homework Effects
Vary With Grade Level?

Yes. The positive effect of homework varied markedly for students at different grade levels—older students benefited most from
doing homework. The average effect of homework was twice as
large for high school as for junior high school students and twice
as large again for junior high as for elementary school students.
Again, to make this finding more precise, teachers of Grades 4, 5,
and 6 might expect the average student doing homework to out-
score about 52% of equivalent no-homework students (there were
very few studies of homework in kindergarten through third
grade). For junior high school students, the equivalent expectation
would be about 60%, and for high school students, about 69%.

What About Other Student Differences?

Comparisons of homework effects on students who differed on
characteristics other than grade level or age generally showed no
difference. Specifically, researchers who have looked at whether

the effects of homework were different for males and females or for students of different intelligence levels have found no differences.

Is Subject Matter Important?

In my literature review, I found that subject matter influenced the outcome of comparisons a bit and in a somewhat unexpected manner. Comparisons involving mathematics revealed the smallest effect of homework; those involving science and social studies revealed the largest effect; and those involving reading and English fell in the middle. When comparisons involving the different subskills of mathematics were made, homework appeared to affect problem solving less than computation or conceptual skills. However, because these findings were not consistent with some other findings described shortly, I prefer to interpret them with caution.

Does Homework Affect All Achievement Measures Equally?

No. How achievement was measured was significantly related to the outcome of homework versus no-homework comparisons. Homework had a larger effect when achievement was measured by class tests or grades than by standardized tests. This seems logical, considering that material on homework assignments should correspond more closely to material that was taught in class and that appeared on class tests than to content covered on more general achievement tests. However, we will see in Chapter 3 that there was no difference between standardized and teacher-developed achievement measures when the effects of time spent on homework is at issue. These studies remind us that the two indices can differ in trustworthiness—standardized measures may be generally more trustworthy than teacher-constructed ones. Thus we might expect the effect of homework to be relatively equal on teacher-developed and standardized measures of achievement, even though the mechanisms producing these results might be quite different.

What About the Frequency
and Length of Assignments?

Not surprisingly, homework produced larger positive effects
if students did more assignments per week. Surprisingly, the effect of homework was negatively related to the duration of the
homework treatment—treatments spanning longer periods produced less of a homework effect. These longer treatments may
have involved less frequent homework assignments during any
given week, thereby lessening its effect.

Does Homework Affect Students' Attitudes?

I have found few studies that involved comparisons of the attitudes of students doing and not doing homework. These studies
suggest that homework has neither a general positive nor negative
effect on students' attitudes toward school, teacher, or subject
matter.

HOMEWORK VERSUS IN-SCHOOL
SUPERVISED STUDY

In the studies reviewed so far, no-homework students received
no instruction meant to compensate for their lack of home study.
In another set of studies, the no-homework students were required
to engage in some form of in-school supervised study not required
of students doing homework. Thus these studies compare the
effects of two different treatments.

The definition of in-school supervised study varied from experiment to experiment. Essentially, three characteristics of the treatment are most germane. First, some researchers have examined
the effects of homework compared with the effects of added study
time at school. This has been accomplished by lengthening the
school day or by shortening the time devoted to subjects or activities not covered in the homework assignments. Second, the type of
supervision given students in the no-homework group has ranged
from passive to active. Sometimes, teachers simply sit and monitor
the study session; other times, they move around the room and

engage students about their work. Finally, supervised study can differ in regard to how closely its content corresponds to that of the students doing homework. In some studies, the content was identical, but in other studies, the material in the two treatments was related but not identical.

My search of the literature located eight studies comparing homework and in-school supervised study. These studies contained 18 comparisons of the two treatments, based on 10 independent samples containing a total of over 1,000 students in 40 classrooms and 10 schools in 6 states. Because this set of comparisons is based on a considerably smaller number of studies than those involving homework and no-homework groups, I was not able to test as many ideas about moderating influences as I was in the prior comparison. Also, these results must be viewed with more caution.

Is Homework Better Than In-School Study?

Generally, yes, that is what the studies indicated, but this overall result can be misleading. Across the 10 independent samples, the average student in the homework condition outperformed about 53.6% of the supervised-study students. This is a smaller effect than was found in comparisons of homework versus no-homework studies. This is not a surprising result given that these studies are really comparing two alternate treatments. It is easy to imagine ways to manipulate homework assignments and/or supervised study so as to produce results favoring one treatment or the other. In addition, the overall result did not hold for all types of students.

Does Grade Level Influence the Effects of the Two Strategies?

Yes. When I compared results according to elementary school (Grades 5 and 6), junior high (Grades 7 to 9), and high school, I found an important relationship. Supervised study had a more positive effect than homework on the achievement of elementary school students, whereas homework was more effective for junior high school and high school students.

What About Subject Matter?

The subject matter considered in a study had no relation to the relative effect of homework versus in-school study. Curiously, the ordering of effects for different subjects was opposite to that for the homework versus no-homework comparisons. Considering this finding and other evidence to be described shortly, I suggest that we should expect larger positive effects of homework on the learning of simple skills that require practice and rehearsal than on complex tasks that require higher-order integration of knowledge and skills. It should be kept in mind, however, that this effect might again be a matter of measurement trustworthiness because simple skills can generally be measured with less error than complex ones. It also does not rule out the use of homework that requires the integration of skills (for example, research reports) or imagination (for example, creative writing). The finding does suggest that such assignments should build on skills that are already well learned.

Is the Type of Achievement Measure Important?

There was no relation between the type of achievement measure used in a study and the comparison's outcome. However, the size of this literature was small, so the tests of difference were weak, and many interesting potential influences could not even be examined.

What About Nonacademic Outcomes?

In two investigations, researchers looked at student attitudes as a function of homework versus in-class supervised study. One study (Hudson, 1965) showed that attitudes toward school were more favorable in the homework treatment-group, whereas the other study (Tupesis, 1972), indicated identical attitudes toward the subject matter expressed by both groups. Although the different results might be explainable by what the attitude question focused on (school vs. subject matter), there are numerous other methodological and context differences between the studies as well.

Finally, one researcher (Hudson, 1965) found better study mechanics and time allocation among students doing homework than doing in-class study. This is the only study I found that used study habits as a measured outcome of homework.

Are After-School Homework Programs Effective?

In recent years, many schools have implemented after-school homework programs. These programs are meant to give students a place to do homework that is conducive to study and where assistance might be available from teachers or other aides. Typically, these programs appear in schools that serve children from poor families, who might not have an appropriate place to study at home or who have working parents who might not be at home after school. So the program provides a safe and supervised environment in addition to homework help.

We might expect that because after-school programs are so much like in-school supervised study, they would show their greatest effectiveness for young children who may be struggling in school—the students for whom most of these programs are developed. Cosden, Morrison, Albanese, and Marcias (in press) recently reviewed the research on after-school programs. First, they found that most after-school programs provide some academic support, but a focus on homework is rare. Furthermore, the designs of programs, because they often include lots of activities in addition to homework help, make it difficult to assess their impact. Cosden and colleagues suggested that the impact of these programs will be influenced by the academic needs of students, the ability of family members to help, who is available to assist with homework in the program, and how often students attend the after-school sessions. Perhaps most encouraging is some evidence that children who attend these programs may experience a boost in self-confidence because they are more likely to complete assignments. Teachers view attendance as a sign of positive motivation, and this may improve their expectations for the student.

GRADE LEVEL, LEARNING DISABILITIES, AND THE VALUE OF HOMEWORK

We have seen that both types of research comparisons revealed that the student's age or grade level influenced the relationship between homework and academic achievement. Homework revealed little or no association with achievement in elementary school. The relationship grew stronger as children matured.

Why Is the Relation Between Homework and Achievement So Weak for Young Children?

To explain the grade-level effect, my colleagues and I turned to the more general literatures in cognitive and developmental psychology (Muhlenbruck, Cooper, Nye, & Lindsay, 2000). First, we found studies indicating that young children have limited attention spans or, more specifically, limited ability to tune out distractions. Thus the distractions at home more easily entice them away from the books spread out on the kitchen table. Second, young children haven't yet learned good study skills. In particular, they don't know how to apportion their time between easy and hard tasks or how to engage in effective self-testing. Each of these cognitive limitations suggests that homework should not be expected to improve test scores impressively and also suggest what might be the most effective home assignments for primary graders. The research also suggests why we found that supervised study is more effective than homework for young children (that is, because someone is present to minimize distractions and assist with proper study).

Should Children With Learning Disabilities Be Assigned Homework?

Educators and parents focus considerable attention on the role of homework in the education of students with learning disabilities. The concern is caused by the fact that students with learning disabilities who attend regular education classes may have difficulty keeping up with regular homework assignments.

When I reviewed the research on homework that had appeared prior to 1986, I found few studies that included students with learning disabilities either as the population of interest or for purposes of comparison to regular-education students. The situation today has improved somewhat. A colleague and I conducted a literature review in 1994 (Cooper & Nye, 1994). We were interested in how homework practices and policies that proved effective for students without disabilities might differ for students with disabilities. Bryan, Burstein, and Bryan (in press) have completed a more recent review.

First, we reviewed studies assessing the overall effectiveness of homework for students with learning disabilities. These studies indicated no reason to believe that the generally positive effects of homework for students without disabilities would not also appear for students with learning disabilities.

Clearly, however, the ingredients of successful homework assignments are different for the two types of students. A consistent theme in the literature is that completing homework assignments is more difficult for students with learning disabilities. This is not just because the same material might be more challenging but also because learning disabilities are often accompanied by other deficits in attention, memory, or organizational skills that, we have seen, influence the success of home study.

These realities suggest that homework assignments for students with learning disabilities should be short and should focus on reinforcement of skills and class lessons, as opposed to integration and extension. Students who fall below a minimum competency in a skill area may not benefit from homework at all.

Close monitoring of homework assignments by teachers is critical for students with learning disabilities. Monitoring might consist of (a) the use of class time to begin assignments so that teachers can ensure that students understand the assignment, (b) frequent contact between teachers and parents to make sure parents understand assignments and that things are going smoothly at home, (c) prompt in-class review, and (d) prominent rewards for completion and accuracy.

Parent involvement is critical for students with disabilities, primarily because these students are likely to have less developed self-management and study skills. Their ability to study depends more on the provision of a proper environment, both physical and emotional. Students with learning disabilities may need periodic rewards during homework time or immediately following assignment completion as well as more assistance in completing tasks. Evidence suggests that this involvement should happen continuously, not periodically.

UNDERSTANDING THE SIZE
OF HOMEWORK'S EFFECT

In the previous sections, I discussed the relative effect of homework across different grade levels, types of outcomes, and content areas. The consequences of homework can also be compared with those of other instructional techniques. This allows us to place homework into a broader educational context, thus permitting a more informed judgment of its value.

The third edition of *Handbook of Research on Teaching* contained an article by Walberg (1986), who presented the results of 11 reviews of research examining the effect of instructional strategies and teaching skills on measures of student achievement. The instructional strategies included individualized, special, and cooperative learning; ability grouping; direct and programmed instruction; advance organizers; higher-level cognitive questioning; use of praise; use of pretests; and watching television. Each strategy had associated with it a measure of effectiveness similar to the one I used previously. Recall that the average student doing homework outperformed 55% of students not doing homework. Based on a comparison with these instructional strategies, the effect of homework on achievement can best be described as *above average*. That is, homework's effect fell in about the middle of the 11 strategies. If grade level is taken into account, homework's effect on achievement of elementary school students could be described as *very small*, but on high school students its effect would be *large*, relative to the effect of other instructional techniques.

Lipsey and Wilson (1993) presented a more exhaustive compendium of research reviews. Here, about 75% of 180 literature reviews of educational practices revealed larger effects than did homework. However, the conclusion of the two comparisons is consistent in that, although the overall impact of homework on achievement might be labeled *small to average*, it was clearly not small for students in secondary school.

Another aid in interpreting the magnitude of an effect is to compare it with the expense of implementing the treatment. Homework certainly can be regarded as a low-cost treatment. The major costs involved in giving homework assignments are (a) a small loss in instructional class time because time must be allocated to homework management, and (b) additional outside-class preparation and management time for teachers.

SUMMARY

In sum, the effect of homework on the achievement of young children appears to be small, even bordering on trivial. However, for high school students the effect of homework can be impressive. Indeed, relative to other instructional techniques and the costs involved in doing it, homework can produce a substantial, positive effect on adolescents' performance in school. In addition, the benefits of homework for students with learning disabilities can be positive, but its success lies in (a) teacher preparation and planning; (b) assignments that are appropriate to the skill, attention, and motivation of students; and (c) successful involvement of parents.

3

Time Spent on Homework Assignments

In the past 40 years, over half a million students have been asked to report the time they spend on homework, and their responses have been related to some measure of academic achievement. Although such surveys can contain a wealth of information, they also have some drawbacks. The major problem is that the results can show that homework and achievement are related but cannot show which, if either, causes the other. It is also possible that a third variable, say, the economic conditions of the communities in which schools are located, causes both the students' achievement and the amount of homework. So if time spent on homework and achievement increase together, does this mean that homework improves school performance, or does it mean that teachers assign more homework to better students? If more homework time is associated with lower achievement, does homework have a detrimental effect on performance, or do brighter students simply finish assignments in less time? Both positive and negative correlations have been found in past research (although positive correlations dominate), and, not surprisingly, each of the four interpretations has been used to make sense of the findings.

Another problem is that most research on time and homework does not distinguish between the amount of homework a teacher assigns and the amount of time a student spends on homework. Finally, studies of time spent on homework typically rely on the self-reports of students. The accuracy of these may be questionable,

because students may be motivated to report doing more homework than they actually do.

This chapter is divided into two main sections. First, the results
of studies are reviewed in which researchers calculated the simple
correlation between time on homework and student achievement
or attitude. As part of this analysis, I examine several influences on
the simple relation, including grade level, subject matter, and how
achievement was measured. Also, I look separately at studies of
whether more time on homework actually causes higher achievement. Second, I examine studies that allowed me to explore
whether there is an optimum amount of homework for students at
different grade levels—that is, whether homework is good up to a
point but then has diminishing effectiveness.

THE SIMPLE RELATION BETWEEN HOMEWORK
TIME AND ACADEMIC OUTCOMES

For my 1989 review, I located 17 studies of the relation between
time on homework and a measure of achievement or attitude. The
studies contained a total of 50 correlations because data were often
analyzed separately for different samples of students, subject matters, grade levels, and outcome measures.

For those readers unfamiliar with correlations, it is necessary to
know only that a correlation, denoted by the symbol r, can range in
value from +1 to –1. A correlation of $r = 0$ means no relationship
exists between time on homework and achievement. If the correlation is positive, it means more time on homework is associated
with higher achievement, and the closer to $r = +1$, the stronger the
relationship. If the correlation is negative, more homework is associated with lower achievement, and $r = -1$ means a perfectly negative association. Generally, a correlation stronger than .30, positive
or negative, is considered moderate in size.

At least six nationwide surveys involving random samples of
students have contained questions about time on homework, including several phases of National Assessment of Educational

Progress, National Assessment in Science, and High School and Beyond. The nationwide surveys have been complemented by statewide surveys conducted in California, North Carolina, Pennsylvania, Rhode Island, and Washington and by numerous school districts. A total of 112,714 students were included in the surveys.

Is Time Spent on Homework Related to Achievement or Attitudes?

Yes. Of the 50 correlations, 43 indicated that students who reported spending more time on homework also scored higher on a measure of achievement or attitude. The average correlation across the studies was $r = +.19$. Figure 3.1 displays the distribution of the 50 correlations, with correlations calculated on elementary, junior high school, and high school students represented by E, J, or S, respectively.

Does Grade Level Have an Effect?

Absolutely. In fact, the most dramatic influence on the time-on-homework and achievement relationship was the grade level of the student. For high school students (Grades 10 to 12), a sizable average correlation was found ($r = +.25$), whereas for students in Grades 6 to 9, the average correlation was small ($r = +.07$), and for elementary school students (Grades 3 to 5), it was nearly nonexistent ($r = +.02$). Figure 3.1 displays this relation by showing the uneven distribution of Es, Js, and Ss across the range of values.

Since the publication of the review, researchers have reported several new studies using large sample sizes. The first of these studies used over 3,000 third- and sixth-grade students from 51 school districts in Indiana (Bents-Hill et al., 1988). The researchers correlated both the number of days parents reported their children did homework and the total time spent on homework with achievement test scores and teacher-assigned grades. For third-grade students, the correlations were negative, ranging from $r = -.22$ to $r = -.09$. For sixth-grade students, the correlations were positive but small, ranging from $r = .00$ to $r = +.15$.

Another study used the 1980 and 1982 High School and Beyond longitudinal database ($N = 25,875$) (Keith & Cool, 1992). Students

Figure 3.1. Distribution of the 50 Correlations Between Time Spent on Homework and Achievement-Related Outcomes

.39,	.40	
.37,	.38	S
.35,	.36	
.33,	.34	J
.31,	.32	
.29,	.30	J
.27,	.28	SS
.25,	.26	JJSS
		S
.23,	.24	JSS
.21,	.22	JJS
.19,	.20	JSSS
.17,	.18	SS
.15,	.16	SS
.13,	.14	JSS
.11,	.12	J
.09,	.10	EJJJ
.07,	.08	EEJ
.05,	.06	EEE
		JS
.03,	.04	
.01,	.02	SS
.00	----	---
−.01,	−.02	E
−.03,	−.04	
−.05,	−.06	EE
−.07,	−.08	J
−.09,	−.10	
−.11,	−.12	E
−.15,	−.16	J
−.17,	−.18	J
−.19,	−.20	

SOURCE: Table adapted from Harris Cooper (1989).
NOTE: Correlations are distinguished by grade level:
    E = Grades 3-5; J = Grades 6-9; S = Grades 10-12.

were tested as sophomores and as seniors. The study found a correlation of $r = +.30$ between time spent on homework and achievement. So the results of these newer studies are consistent with my earlier conclusion that the positive association between time spent on homework and achievement is stronger among older than younger students.

Does the Frequency or Length of Assignments Matter?

I mentioned earlier that most studies of homework simply asked how much time students spend on homework. They did not distinguish between the lengths of any particular assignments or how often (how many times a week) homework is assigned.

We did partially explore this important difference in our survey of teachers, parents, and students. In this study, we asked teachers how much homework they assigned students each night, and we asked students how much of the assignments they completed (Cooper, Lindsay, Nye, & Greathouse, 1998). In lower grades, we found that more homework assigned by teachers each night was associated with less positive attitudes on the part of students. In higher grades, not surprisingly, more assigned homework was associated with less frequent completion of assignments. For all students, completing more homework led to higher grades, even when the students' initial achievement level and the teachers' use of homework in grading were taken into account.

These findings suggest tentatively that homework might be more effective if students are given shorter but more frequent assignments. For example, a third-grade teacher might be advised to assign 30 minutes of homework each night of the week rather than assign 50 minutes of homework on three nights. For young children, this strategy would also be recommended because of their shorter attention span.

Is Subject Matter Important?

Yes. Mathematics produced the strongest average correlation ($r = +.22$), followed by reading ($r = +.20$), and English ($r = +.20$). Science ($r = +.13$) and social studies ($r = +.10$) produced the weakest average correlations. Examining the order of effects leads to an interesting observation; The average correlations get larger for subjects for which homework assignments are more likely to involve rote learning, practice, or rehearsal. Alternatively, subjects such as science and social studies, which often involve longer-term projects, integration of multiple skills, and creative use of nonschool resources show the smallest average correlations. Thinking back to the results described previously, we find three sets of data suggesting that homework may be more effective for learning simple tasks and one data set suggesting the opposite.

Because significant effects were found for both grade level and subject matter, I wanted to see if the two effects were related. To do so, I calculated average correlations for each subject separately for high school and pre-high-school students. As might be expected given previous findings, the effect of subject matter was due entirely to variation among high school students. The pre-high-school correlations were all small, and consistently so across subjects.

What About Achievement Versus Attitudes?

A significant relation was also revealed when the type of outcome measure was examined. Although standardized tests ($r = +.18$) and grades ($r = +.19$) produced nearly identical average correlations, the estimate associated with attitudes was a bit smaller ($r = +.14$). This again may be due to less trustworthy ways of measuring attitudes and interests than achievement. Or, affective and motivational responses to academic work may be less responsive to homework variations. Finally, teachers may not take a positive attitude into account (as much as high achievement) when they decide how much homework to assign. However, although the difference in average correlations is noteworthy, the magnitude of difference is not great.

Do Student Differences Matter?

Regrettably, I found no evidence on whether the relation between time on homework and academic outcomes was influenced by student individual differences. For example, it would be reasonable to expect that some students, perhaps highly academically oriented ones or ones with better study skills, would benefit more from more homework. At this point, however, such assumptions must remain just that, as there is little evidence either to support or refute such claims.

Does Time Spent on Homework Cause Achievement Differences?

Two types of studies have attempted to address the causality question. The first type of study statistically controls for influences that might cause both time spent on homework and achievement and then looks to see if a reliable relationship still exists between the two. The second type of study directly manipulates the time spent on homework and then measures change in achievement.

I found nine studies that statistically controlled for other influences. The controlled variables ranged from pretest scores to ability measures; to the sex, race, and economic background of the student; to classroom and home conditions. The number of controlled variables included in any one analysis ranged from 1 to 16. The results of the nine studies overwhelmingly indicated that the relation between time on homework and achievement remains positive and important. However, in results similar to those concerning the simple relationship, two of the three studies conducted on students in Grades 4, 5, and 6 yielded results suggesting no relationship remained between the two.

In two studies, researchers experimentally varied the amount of homework assigned to students. In one study (Koch, 1965), the amount of homework assigned to three sixth-grade arithmetic classes was determined on a random basis. Conflicting results were found, with math concepts favoring longer homework assignments and problem solving favoring shorter assignments. Another study (Anthony, 1977) involved 18 sections of 9th-, 10th-, and 11th-grade algebra. Each participating teacher taught both one experimental and one control class. A significant effect favoring shorter homework assignments was found. So these studies are also consistent with my earlier suggestion that shorter but more frequent assignments are most effective.

Taken together then, the two experimental studies lend no support to the notion that longer homework assignments lead to higher achievement, at least in mathematics. This result is especially interesting because math generated the largest estimate of relation among the correlational studies described previously. However, firm conclusions cannot be drawn from two small experiments, especially when they appear to contradict another set of studies that involve many more students. What is clear is that we cannot rule out the likelihood that at least some of the relationship between time on homework and achievement found in surveys is due to higher achievement causing more time on homework.

THE CURVILINEAR RELATION BETWEEN HOMEWORK TIME AND ACHIEVEMENT

In addition to studies that contained data estimating simple correlations, I found nine studies that reported levels of achievement for different amounts of time spent on homework. The nine studies included a total of 13 independent samples.

By making some considered assumptions, we could combine these studies to assess the possibility that there was an optimum amount of homework. That is, we could explore the idea that homework had a positive effect on achievement up to a point, but when time spent on homework passed this point, it either resulted in no more improvement or started to have negative effects. Such a curvilinear relation would be consistent with results in related areas. For instance, the relationship between time on task and achievement seems to reach a plateau at which increases in time have only a marginal effect on learning (Frederick & Walberg, 1980). This could also be the case with time on homework.

Is There an Optimum Amount of Homework?

Apparently, yes. But again, it differs from grade to grade. Figure 3.2 presents the results of the analysis for junior high and high school students. It reveals that for high school students, the positive relation between homework time and achievement does not

Figure 3.2. The Curvilinear Relationship Between Time on Homework and Achievement

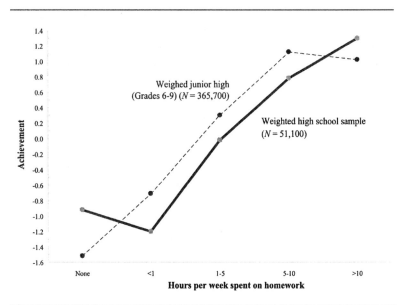

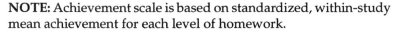

NOTE: Achievement scale is based on standardized, within-study mean achievement for each level of homework.

appear until at least 1 hour of homework per week is reported. Then achievement continues to climb unabated to the highest measured interval, more than 2 hours of homework each night. In contrast, for junior high students the positive relation to achievement appears for even the most minimal level of time on homework (less than 1 hour) but disappears entirely at the highest interval. Only one study was available for Grades 1 through 6 (Hinckley, 1979). It seemed unwise to draw any conclusions about possible curvilinear relations for elementary school students based on a single study.

What About Causality?

Again, because the results are correlational, a causal interpretation of these data can be framed in different ways. For example, it is possible that achievement causes time on homework. If this is the case, then teachers of junior high classes might be advised to use achievement as a guide for how much homework to assign, except for the brightest students. Distinctions in the amount of homework would not be made among the brightest students, at least not based on achievement differences. For high school students, teachers would not use achievement as a basis for determining how much homework to assign to lower achievers, but achievement becomes a causal factor as performance improves.

Another way to construe these data is to view homework as the cause of achievement. When this approach is taken, the data have important implications for homework policies. That is, Figure 3.2 indicates small amounts of homework for high school students are of little utility. However, once a critical amount is reached, perhaps about 1 hour per week, increases in time spent on homework, up to more than 10 hours per week, cause improvement in achievement. No data are available beyond this point. For junior high students, even less than 1 hour of homework a week might improve achievement until between 5 and 10 hours per week are assigned. At this point, there appears to be no advantage to increases in time spent on homework.

SUMMARY

Fifty correlations based on over 112,000 students revealed a positive relation between student reports of time spent on homework and several academic outcomes. Based on these data alone, it is impossible to determine whether more homework causes better achievement, whether teachers assign more homework to students achieving better, or whether better students spend more time on home study. Any or all of these causal relationships are possible. However, in studies in which other explanations for the relationship were ruled out, the positive relationship remained for older students but was not evident before high school. The magnitude of the relationship between time on homework and achievement was influenced by the outcome measure (stronger for achievement than attitudes), the subject matter (stronger for math and reading than science and social studies), and, especially, the grade level of the student (stronger for higher grades). There is also some evidence that shorter but more frequent homework assignments may be more effective than longer, less frequent ones.

Finally, the relation between homework and achievement reached a point of diminishing returns for junior high school students but not for high school students. If homework is taken as the causal agent, the results suggested that increasing the amount of homework for middle-grade students may be a good thing only up to a certain point. High school students can benefit from homework at least up to 2 hours per night. Elementary school students demonstrate little relation between homework and achievement, regardless of the length of assignments.

4

The Homework Assignment

In this chapter, I examine variations in assignments that might be related to the value of homework. First, I consider three general issues related to the content of assignments or to what in Table 1.3 were called initial classroom factors. The questions asked concern (a) whether the content of homework should appear before, after, or concurrently with its discussion in class; (b) whether teachers should individualize homework within classes; and (c) whether homework assignments are better if they are voluntary or required. Then I turn my attention to classroom follow-up in Table 1.3, or different forms of teacher feedback and incentives after assignments are turned in. The questions are related to the homework assignments that have been the focus of past research.

CONTENT OF ASSIGNMENTS

Is the Timing of Homework and Its Related Work in Class Important?

Yes, but let's be clear about definitions. *Same-day-content* homework requires students to do problems that pertain only to material presented in class on the day the problems are assigned. *Distributed* homework assignments include the introduction of material that has not yet been covered in class or that was covered in lessons prior to the current day. In terms of the instructional purposes detailed in Chapter 1, distributed strategies that include material not yet covered are meant as preparation for upcoming topics, whereas coverage of previous material is meant as practice or review.

I found eight studies that examined whether the amount of dispersion of content across homework assignments influences homework's effectiveness. Several studies included measures of the effect of the different strategies not only immediately after the classroom unit was completed but also when a delay occurred between the end of the unit and testing. This permitted an assessment of the strategies in terms of both the short- and long-term retention of material.

All seven studies that included tests of achievement given immediately after the class had completed the content unit revealed that homework assignments including both practice and preparation along with same-day content were superior to assignments that included only same-day content. Specifically, the average student who did preparation, practice, or both types of distributed homework outperformed 54% of students who did only same-day-content homework.

I found two studies that compared preparation homework with current-content homework. They revealed larger differences than the three studies I found that compared practice and current-content homework. This result gives some indication that preparation homework may be more effective than practice homework in increasing students' scores on immediate measures of achievement.

Five studies that included measures of achievement taken sometime after a unit was completed also uniformly indicated that distributed-content homework was more effective than same-day-content homework. In fact, the effect of the different practices was even greater when more time was allowed to pass before the material was tested. The average student in the distributed-homework classrooms scored higher on the delayed measures of achievement than 57% of students in the classrooms who received only same-day-content homework. The one delayed-measurement study that examined a treatment including both preparation and practice homework revealed a larger effect than the four studies that examined one or the other instructional purpose.

Two studies that included preparation homework only did not differ in their result from three studies that included practice homework only, although a trend did again indicate that preparation homework may be more effective than practice homework.

As a whole, the studies of the timing of content were very well designed and, therefore, appear to be trustworthy (for example, treatments were randomly assigned to classes, and students were apparently assigned to classes without bias). However, certain precautions need to be taken in the generalization of these findings. First, no study examined the effect of the timing of homework on students in elementary school. Also, mathematics was the predominant subject of instruction. This said, it is hard to think of a reason why the findings on timing would be different for young children or for subjects other than math.

Do student differences affect preparation or practice homework? I could find none. Four studies that examined whether the effect on achievement of preparation and practice homework was influenced by the intelligence of students revealed no noteworthy difference. Similar results were reported in a study involving student gender and a study in which teachers rated students on how dependent they were on others.

What about attitudes? The two studies that included a measure of student attitudes produced no strong effects. It appears that the timing of homework and related work in class has little effect on students' attitudes toward the covered material.

Should Teachers Individualize Assignments Within a Class?

Generally no, at least not unless they have good reasons associated with particular students or classes. Whether individualizing homework for students at different performance levels improves achievement has been the topic of four studies. Taken together the studies revealed no consistent improvement in achievement when classes with individualized homework were compared to classes in which all students did the same assignment. Two well-conducted studies indicated that the effect of individualization was influenced by numerous other factors, but the influences were not the same from one study to the other. One study compared not only achievement but also the time both students and teachers spent on homework when it was and was not individualized. The results indicated that slower students required more time to complete homework that was not individualized. On the other hand, teachers spent considerably more time constructing and monitoring individualized assignments (Bradley, 1967).

In general, research hints at individualization being effective for some subjects and with certain subgroups of students. Furthermore, logic dictates that individualization would be appropriate in some circumstances, for instance when classes contain students who vary greatly in ability or the amount of prior exposure they have had to the subject matter. However, individualization of homework does not reveal benefits widespread enough to suggest that it be adopted as a matter of general policy. In addition, individualization may significantly increase the time teachers spend preparing and correcting assignments.

Should Homework Be
Compulsory or Voluntary?

In the past 50 years, only one study has compared the effects of compulsory versus voluntary homework. This small study (involving 113 students) found no differences in achievement between the two approaches.

Clearly, however, one can think of circumstances involving high-interest homework in which more academic change might be produced if the assignment were voluntary than if it were required. This reasoning rests on the assumption that if children do things without the presence of obvious external demands, they are more likely to internalize positive sentiments about the activity (see Deci & Ryan, 1985). Also, it is easy to think of circumstances in which voluntary assignments would go undone, making it essential for the assignment to be required if any learning is to take place. It would be imprudent, therefore, to conclude that the two practices had equal effect until larger and more varied studies are conducted.

TEACHER FEEDBACK AND INCENTIVES

The response of teachers when homework assignments are brought back to school can vary in four ways. First, teachers can provide students with instruction on how the assignment could have been completed more accurately. This can be accomplished by reviewing the assigned work with the class as a whole. Or the teacher can provide individual students with written comments describing their accuracy and errors. Second, teachers can give out letter or numerical grades. These grades can then be used as part of the student's overall performance evaluation. Third, teachers can provide praise or criticism, either verbal or written, meant to reward responses that are correct or punish incorrect ones. Both grades and reinforcement can be based simply on whether the homework was completed or on the accuracy of the responses. Finally, teachers can provide nonverbal incentives, such as candy or early dismissal, dependent on the completeness or accuracy of the homework. The four strategies can be applied in combination and with varying frequencies, ranging from continuous to occasional use of any given strategy.

Are Comments and Grading Important to the Utility of Homework?

Surprisingly, I found no study that tested whether the presence versus absence of a feedback strategy influenced the value of homework. Apparently, educators believe the value of such a strategy is so obvious that testing it is unnecessary.

A few studies have involved comparing different strategies to one another. Two studies examined the effects of different types of instructional comments, comparing the strategy of simply telling students an answer was wrong versus describing the type of error. Neither study found a reliable difference on the student's subsequent achievement. One study looked at performance differences between classes that discussed all homework questions versus classes that went over only questions requested by the students.

No differences between the strategies were found. Two studies of evaluative comments (praise or critical remarks vs. no feedback) also showed no effect on the value of homework for improving achievement. Finally, three studies of grading strategies—one comparing grading every math problem versus grading only a random sample of problems, and two comparing grading for completeness versus grading for accuracy—also produced no differences.

What About Providing Incentives?

Studies of the effects of incentives suggest that provision of rewards for handing in homework can increase completion rates. The types of rewards employed have included extra playtime on computers, extra free time, coupons for purchases at the school store, and free-homework passes that allow students to skip future assignments without penalty. Not surprisingly, most of these studies have focused on students with learning disabilities or poor motivation.

SUMMARY

In sum, the eight studies examining practice and preparation homework provide a convincing, consistent pattern favoring these assignment purposes. In fact, distributed assignments have a larger impact on delayed measurement than on immediate measurement of achievement, meaning they may be especially important for promoting retention of material.

Research on variations in feedback strategies reveals little reason to choose one strategy over another. Whether or how much instructional feedback is given, whether all or only some problems are graded, and whether the teacher provides evaluative comments appear to have little relation to homework's effectiveness for improving performance. Finally, there is sound evidence that providing incentives for completion to students who have learning disabilities proves beneficial.

5

Home and Community
Influences on Homework

In the model of influences on homework presented in Table 1.3, I listed three groups of home and community factors: competitors for student time; the home environment; and the involvement of others, especially parents. Competitors for student time, such as watching television, holding an after-school job, or participating in extracurricular and other organized group activities, have been areas of research in their own right. The involvement of parents in the homework process, both by creating a proper home environment and by directly participating in assignments, has been the subject of many homework studies. Several communities have instituted programs that provide after-school telephone assistance to students with homework problems. These programs have never been formally evaluated for their influence on achievement, but a description of one such program gives an idea of how they operate and what might be expected of them.

COMPETITORS FOR STUDENT TIME

Researchers have focused attention on three other after-school activities that compete with homework for a student's time and attention. I briefly describe the evidence on how each relates to school achievement.

Does Watching Television Affect Achievement?

Watching television is an after-school activity widely believed to be associated with lower academic achievement. Television viewing is presumed to lower academic achievement because it replaces academically related activities, such as homework or leisure reading. Others have suggested that television viewing inhibits achievement because it interferes with a child's cognitive development (Anderson & Collins, 1988, as cited in Comstock, 1991).

Some empirical support exists for these assertions. For example, using a national sample from the High School and Beyond Longitudinal Survey, Keith, Reimers, Fehrman, Pottebaum, and Aubey (1986) found a small negative relationship between achievement and the amount of television students said they watched. However, the negative effect of television viewing is not found in every study. So the relationship may be weak and, therefore, sensitive to variations in how it is studied. Indeed, Comstock (1991) concluded that "the evidence indicates a modest causal contribution by television to lesser achievement" (p. 138).

Do High School Students Who Have
After-School Jobs Perform Well in School?

Whether students are employed after school has interested researchers because a large number of students hold jobs. In 1992, almost half of all high school seniors reported being employed (Green, Dugoni, Ingels, & Cambrurn, 1995). Researchers investigating the relationship between employment and achievement have disagreed about whether employment is good or bad for students. To explain this finding, Steinberg, Brown, Cider, Kaczmarek, and Lazzaro (1988) suggested that student employment may relate to academic achievement in a curvilinear fashion. For example, employment may benefit students up to a certain number of hours worked per week. After reaching this number, having a job may begin to interfere with academics.

What About Extracurricular and Other Structured Group Activities?

Many students participate in extracurricular activities. According to the National Educational Longitudinal Study (as cited in Zill, Nord, & Loomis, 1995), approximately 60% of high school sophomores and 70% of seniors participate in at least one extracurricular activity. Yet, despite the plentiful amount of research investigating the academic impact of homework, television, and employment, relatively little attention has been paid to how extracurricular activities shape student academic performance.

Extracurricular activities, such as academic clubs and sports, and other structured after-school activities involving peers, such as scouting or church groups, may directly or indirectly affect a student's academic performance. Directly, we would think that such activities will take time away from studying. However, the indirect effects of some after-school groups and clubs could be positive. Marsh (1992) suggested that participation in extracurricular activities could increase a student's investment in school, which may promote better academic attitudes and habits. In fact, one study has found that among students identified as being at risk for leaving school, the dropout rate was lower for students who participated in extracurricular activities. In general, the research addressing this issue suggests that the relationship between participation in extracurricular activities and achievement may be small but consistently positive.

Summary

We used our survey data to examine the relationship between all of these after-school activities and achievement (Cooper, Valentine, Nye, & Lindsay, 1999). We found that knowing how students spend their nonschool hours can help predict their performance in school. Furthermore, after-school activities that are directly related to achievement (that is, homework) or that foster positive identification with school (for example, extracurricular activities) had positive influences on achievement. Activities that displace schoolwork (for example, television watching) or replace school identities with other identities (for example, employment) had an overall negative influence on achievement.

However, these assertions require strong statements of caution and qualification. First, our data could not be used to make causal claims. Second, we have seen that increasing amounts of homework has positive effects only up to a certain point. A similar limit may prevail for extracurricular activities. Furthermore, watching some television could have benefits for achievement if the content of the viewed programs is related to academics. Finally, depending on the qualifications for the job, employment after school can demonstrate for students that a good education will be necessary if they hope to pursue an attractive profession.

Thus it seems safe to conclude that parents and educators can profitably focus on student after-school activities in general as potentially important influences on achievement. Activities that relate directly to learning or that foster positive school identity, be they homework assignments, clubs, television programs, or jobs exposing students to careers requiring academic skills, can improve achievement. Activities that displace learning or replace school identities with other identities may diminish achievement.

THE HOME ENVIRONMENT AND PARENT INVOLVEMENT

What Can Happen When Parents Become Involved in Homework?

Recall that educators have suggested the impact of parent involvement on the effectiveness of homework could be either positive or negative. First, educators say that parent involvement in home study could be used to accelerate children's learning. But, involvement might also interfere with learning. This could happen if parents are uncomfortable or unable to take on the role of teacher or if parents use instructional techniques different from those being used at school. Second, educators suggest that parent involvement might improve communication between the school and family. Alternatively, direct involvement of parents in homework could lead to excessive pressure on children to complete assignments and do well. This can happen if parents hold expectations for students that are inconsistent with their capabilities. Finally, educators point out that although monitoring and assisting with homework by parents should be beneficial to students, overly involved parents might give assistance beyond tutoring, perhaps by simply giving correct answers or completing assignments themselves.

Complicating the picture further, families differ in the resources of time, space, and materials available to them. This suggests that requests for involvement might be more difficult for families of limited economic means or families in which there is a single parent or multiple children. The results of our survey supported the claim that, although parents report positive experiences with homework most of the time, negative forms of parent involvement in homework occur at least some of the time in most families.

Is Parent Involvement Associated With a Student's Academic Achievement?

Research correlating parent involvement and student achievement suggests no simple relationship. My 1989 literature review found five studies that related the amount of parent involvement to student achievement, with correlations ranging from $r = +.40$ to $r = -.22$. We found two newer large-sample studies that looked at this issue. In the first, Epstein (1988) surveyed first-, third-, and fifth-grade teachers ($n = 82$) and parents ($n = 1,269$) in 16 Maryland school districts. She found negative relationships between the number of minutes parents reported helping with homework and the child's achievement in reading and math. In the second study, T. Keith, P. Keith, Troutman, Bickley, Trivette, and Singh (1993) analyzed the nationally representative sample of 21,814 eighth-grade students and parents taken from the 1988 National Education Longitudinal Study. They used a composite measure of parent involvement that included how often parents checked homework as well as involvement measures not related to homework. They found positive relationships in all subject areas. Part of this association appeared to result from an increase in the amount of homework completed by students with involved parents.

Why Is the Research Inconclusive?

At least two explanations come to mind for the contradictory findings. First, because these studies are correlational, they may be gauging a relationship that goes both ways. That is, it may be the case that both (a) increasing parent involvement causes improved student achievement *and* (b) poor achievement causes greater parent involvement. The latter possibility was supported in the study by Epstein (1988). She found that more parent involvement was associated with lower achievement. However, she also found that parents of low-achieving students said they received from teachers more frequent requests to help, more messages that they should help, and more communications about how to help with homework.

A second explanation for the contradictory findings could be that parent involvement may cause improved student learning under some conditions but interfere with learning under other conditions. Some types of parent help with homework might be beneficial, but other types might be detrimental to student progress.

What Are Some Ways That Parents Can Become Involved in Homework?

Our survey examined a variety of parents' behavior for helping their children with homework and how student, family, and parenting style differences related to student achievement (Cooper, Lindsay, & Nye, in press). We used four dimensions of parenting style to help us understand the role of parents in homework (see Grolnick & Ryan, 1989). *Autonomy support* was defined as how much parents value and use techniques that encourage in their children independent problem solving, choice, and participation in homework decisions. *Direct parent involvement* concerned the extent to which parents are interested in, knowledgeable about, and take an active part in their children's homework assignments. *Provision of structure* referred to the degree to which parents provide clear and consistent guidelines and follow-through on contingencies for their children's homework. Greater structure makes it easier for children to discern who and what controls outcomes. Finally, *interference* refers to how often help from parents actually made homework harder, perhaps because the parent was poor at mentoring or taught material differently from the classroom teacher.

Are Some Types of Parent Involvement More Beneficial Than Others?

The answer to this question appears to be yes. Interestingly, the same behaviors, on the part of a parent, that are helpful with one type of student may be harmful with another, depending on how well the student is doing in school.

We found the four dimensions of parenting style very helpful in interpreting the outcome of our survey. Most important, our results revealed that (a) as a parent's support for autonomy increased, so did the achievement of their child, whereas (b) direct parent involvement, however appropriate, showed the opposite relationship with these same outcomes. I find it unlikely that a high level of direct parent involvement—for example, requests for help from the teacher or student—is very often the cause of poorer student achievement. Instead, I suspect that the mechanism underlying our findings involves parents choosing their type of involvement in homework based on how well their child is doing in school. If the student is performing relatively poorly in school, the parent (often at the urging of the teacher) may become more directly involved in the performance of homework. If the student is doing well in school, parents may shift their focus to providing autonomy support or leaving the student alone to do homework and letting the student play a more active role in determining when and how homework is completed.

Does Grade Level Make a Difference?

Again, yes, we found some interesting developmental differences. Homework content in elementary school is not difficult, and most parents ought to possess the knowledge required to be effective teachers at home. Therefore parents of young students may reveal their most important differences in how much independence they provide their children. Material becomes more complex as students move along in school. So for older students good mentoring skills might involve both the provision of autonomy and, independently, the parents' refraining from providing help that actually interferes with their children's studying. These notions were supported by our findings that having a student in the upper-grade levels was associated with parent reports of both more autonomy training and less effective attempts at help.

What About the Parents' Role in Creating a Good Environment for Doing Homework?

In our survey, not surprisingly, parents reported they were less able to eliminate distractions from their children's environment when an adult was not at home after school. For elementary school students, creating a good homework environment was also more difficult when there were more children living in the home. Generally, we would expect that as the number of brothers and sisters increases, the parent and family resources available for involvement with any single child increases. Thinking about families as varying in resources available to support children's homework and, indeed, their education in general provides a valuable framework for understanding several findings relating parenting style to family differences in homework process.

Do Homework Hotlines and Web Sites Help?

One type of community-based effort related to homework involves the establishment of homework hotlines. These are telephone services in which teachers or other knowledgeable people are available to answer questions related to homework problems. The idea behind the service is to help callers who do not have available at home the resources necessary to solve problems encountered in homework or who might have forgotten the procedure needed to complete an assignment. Other schools and individual teachers have set up Web sites that are meant to provide similar help, although these rarely involve real-time interaction between students and teachers or other tutors.

It is difficult to assess the effectiveness of such programs using the outcome variables that appear in other types of homework research. However, logic suggests that in some school districts, especially large ones, the hotlines and Web sites might be of some service and be run in a cost-effective manner. Experience suggests, however, that students need to be kept aware that the program exists or else the initial enthusiasm surrounding them can disappear.

Summary

What, then, are the implications for teachers and parents of research on parent involvement in homework? First, teachers should be cautious in requesting that parents provide active instruction to their students. In making such requests, teachers should consider whether the families they serve generally have the needed economic, time, and skill resources. In determining parental skill levels, teachers should consider both the difficulty of the homework assignment and the educational background of the parents. When parent-skill resources are low, teachers might consider employing a program that trains parents in how to be effective facilitators, such as the Teachers Involve Parents in Schoolwork (TIPS) program (Epstein & Dauber, 1989).

Second, teachers and parents should consider the ability level of the student in determining what role the parent should play in homework. Our results are consistent with the suggestion that an active teaching role for parents may be most appropriate for students in early grades who may be experiencing difficulty in school. However, because training students to be autonomous learners may improve later achievement, parents of students who are doing well in school should be encouraged not to interfere with self-study. Proponents have pointed out that one of the major benefits of homework is its ability to help students develop time-management and study skills and to become autonomous, lifelong learners outside formal educational settings.

6

Homework Policies for School Districts, Schools, and Classrooms

Given the importance of homework in schooling, it is surprising to discover how few school districts have homework policies. Roderique, Polloway, Cumblad, Epstein, and Bursuck (1994) conducted a national survey of school districts and found that only 35% had written homework policies. Similar results were found in surveys of high schools in Illinois and of chief school-administrators in Pennsylvania.

In this chapter, I examine the topic of homework policies for school districts, schools, and classrooms. First, I summarize the results of a survey of the content of school district homework policies. Then I present some policy advice provided by a government agency and three not-for-profit national organizations. In each case, I look at whether these policy suggestions are consistent with research findings. Finally, I conclude the chapter with a set of general policy statements that can serve as a starting point for districts, schools, and classrooms considering developing new policies or revising existing ones.

CURRENT POLICIES OF SCHOOL DISTRICTS

Roderique and colleagues (1994) sent questionnaires about homework policies to 550 randomly chosen school districts. They received 267 responses. These responses indicated that among the one third of school districts that had homework policies, 4 in 5 said following the policy was not required of teachers. About two thirds of school districts with policies said they permitted modification of their general policy for students with learning disabilities, with modifications to be based on the needs of the student and the discretion of the teacher.

Some school districts included regulations in their policy regarding the frequency and length of assignments. These regulations were more likely to refer to elementary school homework assignments than to middle school and high school ones. Among those school districts that included policies on amount of homework, the typical school-district policy suggested that elementary schools assign homework three or four times a week, middle schools four times a week, and high schools four or five times a week. The average amount of recommended homework per night ranged from about 40 minutes in elementary school to 70 minutes in middle school to 100 minutes in high school.

Half of the school districts specified the type of homework that should be assigned. Among these, preparation assignments (that is, ones that help students get ready for material about to be discussed in class) were prescribed most often. About half of the districts also specified the type of feedback to be given on assignments.

Nine in 10 districts said they informed parents about the policy. About half of the written policies included material that covered the role of parents in the homework process. The most frequently mentioned roles for parents, in descending order, were these: provide space, monitor task completion, monitor time allocation, assist with work completion, provide enrichment activities, help study for tests, sign completed work, tutor specific skills, and provide consequences.

In sum then, the surveys of school districts suggest that most districts have no policy whatsoever. Among those that do, the typical regulations that appear in them are largely consistent with the research findings. Specifically, the developmental differences that researchers find in children's ability to profit from homework are recognized in the suggested frequency and length of assignments. Modifications are made for students with learning disabilities. Teachers are required to keep parents informed. The roles for parents are defined primarily as providing structure and monitoring and secondarily as providing direct assistance or instruction. An emphasis is placed on distributing the content of assignments rather than massing it on the day that the content is covered in class. A school district can adopt any or all of these prescriptions and make a legitimate claim that they are based on the best research evidence available.

THE DEPARTMENT OF EDUCATION'S *WHAT WORKS*

One of the most popular publications ever printed by the U.S. government is a booklet titled *What Works* (U.S. Department of Education, 1986). *What Works* was intended to be a distillation of research on teaching and learning. Not surprisingly, it contains sections that relate to both the quantity and quality of homework assignments. Figure 6.1 reproduces the section on homework quantity in *What Works.*

Based on the findings of my literature review, there is a major qualifier to the assertion in *What Works* that amount of homework and student achievement are positively related—it applies only to high school students. The graphs in Figure 6.1 portray a linear relation between the amount of homework a student reports doing each week and achievement scores. My review showed that junior high school students doing 5 to 10 hours of homework a week performed no better on achievement tests than students doing 1 to 5 hours. In Grades 4 to 6, there was no meaningful relation between time on homework and achievement. No data exist for lower-level elementary school grades.

The comments in Figure 6.1 seem justifiable. The first paragraph contains an easily understood description of homework's effect size (based on results of a single study). The next paragraph includes a reasonable theoretical rationale for the homework-achievement link. The third paragraph points out that teachers report assigning more homework than students report doing.

Figure 6.1. *What Works* on the Quantity of Homework

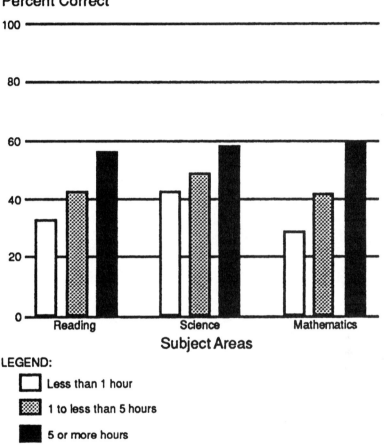

SOURCE: U. S. Department of Education, National Center for Educational Statistics (1985).

In sum, the implications of *What Works* for policies regarding high school are sound. However, if applied to other grades, they may be misleading. They do not take into account the differences between young and older students in their ability to profit from self-study.

Figure 6.2 contains the section in *What Works* on the quality of homework. The paragraph on the research findings suffers from a vague description of homework's effect. No outcome measure is mentioned for gauging the influence of well-designed homework, that is, assignments that are carefully prepared, thoroughly explained, and promptly commented on. The comment is more specific. However, my review of research indicates that only one outcome appears to have withstood empirical testing: Well-designed homework is more likely to be completed than homework that is not well designed. The nonacademic effects cited in the second and third paragraphs have never been the focus of research.

The authors of *What Works* avoid making assertions about the effect of well-designed homework on achievement. Of the several components of well-designed homework, only comments and criticisms have been tested for their influence on test scores. However, in these studies, researchers examined different feedback strategies rather than the presence versus absence of feedback per se.

THE PTA AND THE NEA

The National Parent Teacher Association (PTA) and the National Education Association (NEA) have jointly produced an online homework guide titled *Helping Your Student Get the Most Out of Homework* (Henderson, 1996), which contains the following statement:

> Most educators agree that for children in grades K-2, homework is most effective when it does not exceed 10-20 minutes each day; older children, in grades 3-6, can handle 30-60 minutes a day; in junior and senior high school the amount of homework will vary by subject. Most older students will also have homework projects, such as research papers and oral reports, that may have deadlines weeks away.

(text continues on page 57)

Figure 6.2. *What Works* on the Quality of Homework

Homework: Quality

Research Finding: **Well-designed homework assignments relate directly to class work and extend students' learning beyond the classroom. Homework is most useful when teachers carefully prepare the assignment, thoroughly explain it, and give prompt comments and criticism when the work is completed.**

Comment: To make the most of what students learn from doing homework, teachers need to give the same care to preparing homework assignments as they give to classroom instruction. When teachers prepare written instructions and discuss homework assignments with students, they find their students take the homework more seriously than if the assignments are simply announced. Students are more willing to do homework when they believe it is useful, when teachers treat it as an integral part of instruction, when it is evaluated by the teacher, and when it counts as a part of the grade.

Assignments that require students to think and are, therefore, more interesting, foster their desire to learn both in and out of school. Such activities include explaining what is seen or read in class; comparing, relating, and experimenting with ideas; and analyzing principles.

Effective homework assignments do not just supplement the classroom lesson; they also teach students to be independent learners. Homework gives students experience in following directions, making judgments and comparisons, raising additional questions for study, and developing responsibility and self-discipline.

References: Austin, J. (1976). "Do Comments on Mathematics Homework Affect Student Achievement?" *School Science and Mathematics,* Vol. 76, No. 2, pp. 159-164.
Coulter, F. (1980). "Secondary School Homework: Cooperative Research Study Report No. 7." (ERIC Document Reproduction Service No. ED 209200)
Dick, D. (1980). "An Experimental Study of the Effects of Required Homework Review Versus Review on Request Upon Achievement." (ERIC Document Reproduction Service No. ED 194320)
Featherstone, H. (1995, February). "Homework." *The Harvard Education Letter.*
Walberg, H. J. (1985, April). "Homework's Powerful Effects on Learning." *Educational Leadership,* Vol. 42, No. 7, pp. 76-79.

(continued)

Figure 6.2. *What Works* on the Quality of Homework (*continued*)

Homework: Quantity

Research Finding: **Student achievement rises significantly when teachers regularly assign homework and students conscientously do it.**

Comment: Extra studying helps children at all levels of ability. One research study reveals that when low-ability students do just 1 to 3 hours of homework a week, their grades are usually as high as those of average-ability students who do not do homework. Similarly, when average-ability students do 3 to 5 hours of homework a week, their grades usually equal those of high-ability students who do not do homework.

Homework boosts achievement because the total time spent studying influences how much is learned. Low-achieving high school students study less than high achievers and do less homework. Time is not the only ingredient of learning, but without it little can be achieved.

Teachers, parents, and students determine how much, how useful, and how good the homework is. On average, American teachers say they assign about 10 hours of homework each week—about 2 hours per school day. But high school seniors report they spend only 4 to 5 hours a week doing homework, and 10 percent say they do none at all or have none assigned. In contrast, students in Japan spend about twice as much time studying outside school as American students.

References: Coleman, J. S., Hoffer, T., and Kilgore, S. (1982). *High School Achievement: Public, Catholic and Private Schools Compared.* New York: Basic Books.
Keith, T. Z. (April 1982). "Time Spent on Homework and High School Grades: A Large-Sample Path Analysis." *Journal of Educational Psychology,* Vol. 74, No. 2, pp. 248-253.
National Center for Educational Statistics. (April 1983). *School District Survey of Academic Requirements and Achievement.* Washington, D. C.: U. S. Department of Education, Fast Response Survey Systems. ERIC Document No. ED 238097.
Rohlen, T. P. (1983). *Japan's High Schools.* Berkeley, CA: University of California Press.
Walberg, H. J. (1984). "Improving the Productivity of America's Schools." *Educational Leadership,* Vol. 41, No. 8, pp. 19-36

These recommendations clearly are consistent with the conclusions reached by my combined analyses of dozens of studies. They incorporate what we know about the development of longer attention spans and better study skills as children mature.

The PTA and NEA guide also contains the statement "Research shows that when homework is turned in to the teacher, graded, and discussed with students, it can improve students' grades and understanding of their schoolwork." This statement is less defensible as a research conclusion, primarily because of the reference to the role that grading is suggested to play in determining the effectiveness of homework assignments. My review found no studies of the effects of grading or evaluative comments versus no grading or comments on the effectiveness of homework. The existing research indicates that different strategies for providing feedback vary little in their influence on achievement. Realistically, it seems that students might not take assignments seriously or might not complete them at all if they are not going to be monitored either through grading or some penalty for failure to turn in the work. The evidence suggests, however, that intermittent grading and comments are no less effective than providing continuous feedback. Therefore, I suggest that the practice of grading homework be kept to a minimum, especially if the assignment's purpose is to foster positive attitudes toward the subject matter. Grading might provide external reasons for doing homework that detract from students' appreciation of the intrinsic value of the exercise.

This does not mean that homework assignments should go unmonitored. All homework should be collected, and teachers should use it in the diagnosis of learning difficulties. If a teacher notices a student falling behind in class, homework assignments can be carefully scrutinized to determine where the difficulty lies. When errors or misunderstandings on homework are found, the teacher should more carefully go over the student's other assignments. Problems can then be communicated directly to the student. In a sense, then, homework can help teachers individualize instruction. There is no more reason to treat each homework assignment as if it were a test than there is reason to grade students for their performance on each class lesson.

KAPPA DELTA PI

Kappa Delta Pi, the international honor society in education, publishes a series of booklets on classroom practices. One booklet, *Homework*, is by Timothy Keith (1986). The issues Keith focuses on are time, grade level, subject matter, and quality. Figure 6.3 presents excerpts on each.

Keith's general recommendations regarding the amount of time students should spend on homework reflect the research finding that homework is more beneficial at higher grades. However, the results of my research review are somewhat at odds with his time recommendations, especially for upper-elementary and junior high school students. Considering the generally small effects of homework on achievement in fourth through sixth grade, an upper range of 90 minutes of homework per night may be excessive for many 10-to-12-year olds, unless these assignments contain material of very high interest to the student. Likewise, the data indicate that students in seventh through ninth grade doing 1 hour of homework per night perform as well as students doing closer to 2 hours.

If homework has no noticeable effect on achievement in elementary school grades, why assign any at all? Keith's comments on grade level and parent involvement hint at what I think is the primary rationale. In earlier grades, students can be given homework assignments meant not to produce dramatic gains in achievement but, rather, to promote good attitudes and study habits, dispel the notion that learning occurs only in school, and allow parents the opportunity to express to children how much they value education. For such effects to occur, it seems crucial that assignments be short and simple. Of course, there is as yet no research evidence to support or refute whether the recommended types of homework for elementary school children actually have the intended effects.

With regard to subject matter, Keith points out the subtle differences in content that may lie behind the fact that homework has different effects for different subjects. He suggests that math and spelling lend themselves to practice assignments. My review

(text continues on page 61)

Figure 6.3. Excerpts From Keith (1986) on Homework

Time:	Much will depend on the individual community, the individual school teacher, and even the individual student. Nevertheless, the following time ranges, geared toward the average student should be workable for many situations. • 10 to 45 minutes per night in Grades 1 to 3. • 45 to 90 minutes per night in Grades 4 to 6. • 1 to 2 hours per night for Grades 7 through 9. • 90 minutes to 2½ hours per night for Grades 10 through 12. (p. 17)
Grade Level:	Types of homework assigned should change, at least in proportion, as children grow older. If the types of homework are considered a hierarchy, from practice at the lowest level to creative at the highest, it seems apparent that, in general, the proportion of higher level homework should increase with grade level. (p. 14)
Subject Matter:	Math and Spelling, for example, lend themselves to practice assignments, especially in the early grades, but a class in Literature would seem to lend itself to preparation and creative homework. But again, there is much room for variation, depending on the purpose, the particular topic being covered, and the grade level of the students. (p. 17)
Quality:	The purposes of the assignment should be clear, to the teacher and to the students, as should the notion of how the students should profit and what they should learn from the assignment. The tasks assigned should be relevant to what the children are learning in school, and the assignment type should be appropriate for the purposes, the grade, and the subject matter. Finally, there should be some review or reinforcement of assignments so that homework is not a dead end. If the tasks assigned as homework have a worthwhile purpose in the first

(continued)

Figure 6.3. Excerpts From Keith (1986) on Homework (*continued*)

	place, they should certainly be worth following up in class. (p. 19) It is often wise to start a homework assignment in class to make sure students understand the assignment and are getting off on the right foot. This practice will be especially important for less able students or when students in the class are completing different assignments. (p. 20)
Individual- ization:	In many cases, homework may offer an opportunity to provide some differential, or individualized, instruction. This does not mean that every child in the class needs a different homework assignment every night. On the other hand, it is quite possible to vary the difficulty level, and at times even the assignment type, for those students in the class who seem unlikely to benefit from the assignment as given. (p. 20)
Parent Involvement:	The wisest course would seem to be to keep parental involvement to a minimum (Rosemond, 1984). Parents should provide a quiet place for their children to study, even if only the kitchen table. They should provide the structure and the encouragement to help the child complete the assignment, and they should convey that they feel the completion of homework (and learning in general) is important. . . . Parents should also be available to help with an occasional question if they feel comfortable in this role, and should be available to review completed assignments if there is time (Rosemond, 1984). (p. 22) Again, although extensive involvement may be helpful on occasion, minimal involvement in actual homework should be the rule; parents should be encouraged to remember that it is their *child's* homework, not theirs. . . . As with any rule, there are exceptions. And the parental involvement rule should probably be relaxed with elementary students. (p. 23)

Figure 6.3. Excerpts From Keith (1986) on Homework *(continued)*

Feedback:	Once students have completed homework, their work should be evaluated in some way. This generally means collecting, evaluating, and returning their assignments. . . . Although not every assignment must be graded, it is good to remember that homework that is graded or commented on seems to produce higher achievement than homework that is ungraded (Paschal et al., 1984). Thus graded homework should be the norm. . . . Comments, particularly *positive* comments, on students' papers will also produce better learning (cf., Austin, 1976; Page, 1958; Paschal, 1984), as well as demonstrating that you think homework is important. (p. 28)

SOURCE: Keith (1986).

found that subjects and topics suited to practice- and preparation-type assignments also showed the strongest relation between homework and achievement. Based on this reasoning, I interpreted the research as suggesting that homework may be most effective for the learning of simple tasks. However, if the purpose of homework is to generate interest in a topic, assignments should be more challenging, requiring the use of higher-order thinking skills and the integration of different domains of knowledge.

The main message of my review of homework research regarding both grade level and content is clear. Teachers should not assign homework to young children with the expectation that it will noticeably enhance achievement test-scores. Nor should they expect students to be capable of teaching themselves complex skills at home. Instead, teachers might assign short and simple homework to younger students, hoping it will foster positive, long-term, education-related behaviors and attitudes. Students should be given simple assignments to improve achievement and complex assignments to generate interest in the subject matter.

Keith's recommendations regarding the quality of homework mirror those made in *What Works*. Again, the suggestions make good sense although a research base for them is lacking. Keith also neglects to mention the value of distributing the content of homework across multiple assignments.

Although Keith's recommendation concerning individualization, that is, tailoring assignments for each student within a class, seems harmless, teachers and parents should not expect great benefits to accrue from the practice. The research suggests that individualized homework for students in the same class will rarely prove more effective than well-constructed group or class assignments. This statement is based on the assumption that most classrooms have students at roughly the same ability level. To the extent that learning skills are not the same, individualization might take on some added value. In earlier grades, assignments should be short and simple enough so that they pose no great difficulty to any student, even though the time required to complete them will vary from student to student. At more advanced grade levels, choice in class selection usually produces similar groups of students, but, on average, the groups may differ. In such cases, different homework assignments for various classes are certainly called for. Furthermore, if teachers teach, for example, one average and one accelerated class, they might consider having the brightest students in the average class do portions of the homework assigned to the accelerated group.

Keith's suggestions concerning parent involvement appear to be supported by research. Studies examining whether there are positive effects to casting parents in the role of teacher suggest this will be of limited success. Parents may be most effective as teachers when children are young or struggling in school. However, it makes good sense to have parents play a supportive role in the homework process, no matter the age or achievement level of the child. Teachers should encourage all parents to take part in supportive but indirect ways.

Finally, as detailed above, Keith's recommendations (and those of many others) concerning grading of homework are not based on research findings. I could find no research comparing grading of assignments to no grading, and studies comparing alternate feedback strategies find little difference between them in effectiveness.

In sum, Keith's homework guidelines are generally consistent with the research findings, with four exceptions. First, his ranges for appropriate amounts of time spent on homework may be too long. I suggest that his lower range serve as an average. Second, I would be more explicit about the different purposes of homework for students at different grades. Third, Keith omits the distribution of content across assignments as a key element of quality homework. Fourth, Keith endorses the use of grading and evaluative comments on homework assignments. Research on this issue is minimal. I view homework more as a diagnostic device than an opportunity to test. Furthermore, the grading of homework may severely limit its ability to foster positive attitudes toward the material.

OTHER SOURCES OF POLICY GUIDELINES

The policy guides I have examined include the major issues that need to be addressed when a district, school, or teacher decides to develop a policy on homework. The federal government and national organizations, however, are not the only ones who issue guidelines. I would recommend especially that groups searching for policy suggestions contact state departments and boards of education. Some states provide complete kits that cover not only what to include in policies but also suggest a process for arriving at a policy. Searching the Department of Education's ERIC reference database can provide access to these materials as well as a wealth of other information.

Also, examples of homework policies are obtainable from school districts and even individual schools. From the letters I received while conducting my review, it was obvious that many schools and districts take great pride in the care and thoroughness with which their policies have been constructed.

POLICY STATEMENTS BASED
ON THE PRESENT REVIEW

We have seen that most school districts have no homework policy. My experience suggests that many of the districts that do have policies created them in response to a controversy in their community over the assignment of too much or too little homework. Generally, it is bad practice to develop policies in an atmosphere of contention.

Furthermore, homework policies should exist at the district, school, and classroom levels. The issues addressed at each level are generally different, although they certainly overlap.

What Should Be Contained in
District Homework Policies?

For school districts, the level of detail of a homework policy should not be great, but the policy should address the general purposes and expectations about homework. A policy should at least contain a succinct statement indicating that homework is a cost-effective instructional technique that should have a positive effect on student achievement. The policy should also state that homework may also have some unique benefits for the general character development of children. Finally, homework may serve as a vital link between schools, families, and the broader community.

It is also important that district policies address three substantive issues. These guides would be meant to prevent the wide variations in practices from one school to another that so often cause trouble for administrators and teachers. However, the recommendations should be broad enough so that schools and classrooms have flexibility to respond to local conditions.

First, my recommendation is that districts adopt a policy that requires some homework to be assigned at all grade levels but recognizes that a mixture of both mandatory and voluntary assignments may be most beneficial to students.

Second, districts should prescribe general ranges for the frequency and duration of assignments. These ought to reflect the grade-level differences mentioned previously but should also be influenced by community factors. Such guidelines for a nationally representative, or generic, district might be:

Grades 1-3—three to four mandatory assignments per week, each lasting no more than 10 to 30 minutes.

Grades 4-6—three to four mandatory assignments per week, each lasting between 40 and 60 minutes.

Grades 7-9—four to five mandatory assignments per week, each lasting between 70 and 90 minutes for all subjects combined.

Grades 10-12—four to five mandatory assignments per week, each lasting between 100 and 120 minutes for all subjects combined.

Alternatively, a district might adopt what educators refer to as the *10-minute rule*. The rule conveys to students and parents that each night they should expect all homework assignments together to last about as long as 10 minutes multiplied by the student's grade level. So first graders could expect 10 minutes per night, second graders could expect 20 minutes, third graders 30 minutes, and so on. This rule is attractive because it is simple to communicate while also being consistent with research regarding both the length and frequency of assignments.

I have often been asked whether suggestions about time on homework include required reading time. There exists no research literature on the combined effects of length and subject matter of assignments. My response has been to suggest that the length of nightly homework assignments might be modified upward a bit—perhaps a *15-minute rule*—if the covered material is of high interest to students, regardless of the skill area involved. My sense is that pushing beyond a 15-minute rule, generally speaking, creates situations in which the costs of homework will begin to outweigh the benefits.

Finally, district policies need to acknowledge that homework should serve different purposes at varying grades. For younger students, homework should be used to reinforce the basic skills learned in class, foster positive attitudes toward school, and improve academic-related behaviors and character traits but not primarily to improve or accelerate subject-matter achievement. As students grow older, the function of homework should gradually change toward facilitating the acquisition of knowledge in specific topics.

What Should Be Contained in School Policies?

A school homework policy might further specify the time ranges for different grade levels and subjects. This is especially important in schools where different teachers teach different subjects. A scheme must be adopted so that each teacher knows (a) what days of the week are available to him/her for homework assignments and (b) how much of the students' total daily homework time is allocated to that subject. It is important to have such a policy even if the policy states that no coordination across classrooms will occur, so students can expect varying amounts of homework on different nights. Stating a hands-off policy is important because it sets out what the expectation is and the educational reason for it.

School policies should also contain guidelines that describe the roles of administrators in the homework process. Included in the administrative guidelines should be (a) communicating the district and school policy to parents, (b) monitoring the implementation of the policy, and (c) coordinating the scheduling of homework among different teachers, if needed.

Whether or not guidelines for teachers should be included in schoolwide homework policies is a decision best made at each school. Some teachers might view such policies as unnecessary intrusions on their professional judgment. Others might perceive them as opportunities to learn from the experience of other teachers and to foster a strong community spirit in the school.

I recommend that schoolwide policies relating to the role of the teacher focus primarily on the design of high-quality assignments. Among these recommendations would be that teachers clearly state (a) how the assignment is related to the topic under study, (b) the purpose of the assignment, (c) how the assignment might best be carried out, and (d) what the student needs to do to demonstrate that the assignment has been completed. It is also important that teachers ensure that students have available the necessary resources to carry out an assignment.

What Should Be Contained in Classroom Policies?

Teachers need to adopt a policy governing homework in their classes. Based on the research findings, a nationally representative classroom might include the following points in a policy:

- The length and frequency of homework assignments will be determined by the developmental stage of the students, including their ability level, and by the resources available in homes.
- Amounts of homework will be within the guidelines set out by the school and school district but will also reflect the unique characteristics of the students and families served by the class.
- Assignments will generally be the same for all students in the class or learning group. Although individualization may occur, it will be the exception rather than the rule. Choice and individualization in homework will occur through the provision of voluntary assignments of high interest to students.
- Homework will have content that includes topics that appear in assignments before and after they are covered in class. Some homework assignments will involve practicing skills that are learned by rote (for example, spelling, math facts, foreign languages). Some assignments will attempt to demonstrate to students that the things they learn in school have applications to activities they enjoy doing at home.
- Homework will not be used to teach complex skills and material. If the purpose of homework is to enhance achievement, especially in the early grades, it will generally focus on the reinforcement of simple skills and material. More complex tasks (for example, writing compositions or research reports) can be valuable assignments but should generally require the integration of skills students already possess.
- Parents will rarely be asked to assist in homework in a formal instructional role. When this does occur, the teacher will consider the time and skill resources of parents. All parents can expect that their help will be recruited to ensure that the home environment makes it easy for their child to engage in self-study.

- The teacher will not formally evaluate or grade each homework assignment. Although it would be ideal for all assignments to be carefully scrutinized, time constraints might not make this possible. The teacher will scan students' work to get a sense of whether they have taken the assignment seriously. If homework indicates that a student does not understand the concepts or has not mastered the skills, it will be used to help guide interactive instruction between the teacher and the student.

SUMMARY

Figure 6.4 contains a summary of the kinds of statements that might be included in policies for school districts, schools, and classrooms. It is important to emphasize that the general guidelines I offer are not applicable to all districts, schools, and classrooms. They need to be adapted to meet local conditions. They also might be supplemented with recommendations concerning other aspects of homework, for example, the role of group and long-term projects. What my guidelines are is a set of general suggestions concerning those aspects of policy that can be informed by cumulative, empirical research and sound judgment.

Figure 6.4. Summary of Homework Policy Guidelines

FOR DISTRICTS

Homework is a cost-effective instructional technique. It can have positive effects on achievement and character development and can serve as a vital link between the school and family.

Homework should have different purposes at different grades. For younger students, it should foster positive attitudes, habits, and character traits and reinforce the learning of simple skills introduced in class. For older students, it should facilitate knowledge acquisition in specific topics.

Homework should be required at all grade levels, but a mixture of mandatory and voluntary homework is most beneficial.

The frequency and duration of mandatory assignments should be as follows:
Grades 1 to 3—three to four assignments per week, each lasting no more than 10 to 30 minutes
Grades 4 to 6—three to four assignments per week, each lasting 40 to 60 minutes
Grades 7 to 9—four to five assignments, each lasting 70 to 90 minutes for all aspects combined
Grades 10 to 12—four to five assignments per week, each lasting 100 to 120 minutes for all subjects combined

FOR SCHOOLS

The frequency and duration of homework assignments can be further specified to reflect local school and neighborhood circumstances.

(continued)

Figure 6.4. Summary of Homework Policy Guidelines (*continued*)

In schools where different subjects are taught by different teachers, teachers should know
  1. What days of the week are available to them for assignments
  2. How much daily homework time should be spent on their subject

Administrators should
  1. Communicate the district and school homework policies to parents
  2. Monitor the implementation of the policy
  3. Coordinate the scheduling of homework among different subjects, if needed

Teachers should state clearly
  1. How the assignment is related to the topic under study
  2. The purpose of the assignment
  3. How the assignment might best be carried out
  4. What the student needs to do to demonstrate the assignment has been completed

FOR CLASSROOMS

The length and frequency of homework assignments will take into account the developmental level of students in the class as well as the resources available in their homes.

All students in a class will be responsible for the same assignments, with rare exception. Homework will include both mandatory and voluntary assignments.

(continued)

Figure 6.4. Summary of Homework Policy Guidelines (*continued*)

Topics will appear in assignments before and after they are covered in class, not just on the day they are discussed. Students can expect assignments that help them practice skills already learned, prepare them to learn new skills in class, and require them to apply learned skills to new situations outside of school.

Homework will not be used to teach complex skills. It will generally focus on skills and material already learned, on extending these skills, or on the integration of skills already possessed by the student.

Parents will rarely be asked to play a formal instructional role in homework. Instead, they will be asked to create a home environment that facilitates student self-study.

All homework assignments will *not* be formally evaluated. They will be used to locate problems in student progress and to individualize instruction.

7

Quick Tips for
Parents and Students

In Chapter 6, I examined a few sets of policy recommendations in terms of how consistent they were with the outcomes of research. Then I suggested some statements that reflected what we know to be the best homework policies for school districts, schools, and classrooms. In this chapter, I turn to issues in the homework process from the perspective of parents and students. Put differently, I try to distill from the research some suggestions for parents and students about how best to complete assignments and how to handle difficulties when they arise. As in the previous chapter, I use some materials developed by government and nonprofit organizations to help me focus my discussion.

THE PTA AND THE NEA

The National Parent Teacher Association (PTA) and the National Education Association (NEA) online homework guide titled *Helping Your Student Get the Most Out of Homework* (Henderson, 1996) contains numerous suggestions for parents. Presented in a question-and-answer format, it includes such questions as "How can I help with homework?" Seven suggestions follow.

1. Send your children to school each day well rested, fed, and with a positive outlook.

2. Take an active interest in your children's schooling.

3. Try not to let your own negative experiences keep you from supporting and encouraging your children's learning.

4. If possible, set up a quiet, comfortable study area with good lighting and the school supplies that your children need.

5. Set a family quiet time during which you and your children can work together on homework, reading, letter writing, and playing games.

6. Allow your children to study in a way that helps each of them learn best.

7. Make homework a daily activity and help your children develop good homework habits.

Most of these suggestions are supported by common sense and by what we know about general ways to develop good habits in children. From the homework research, we can emphasize the third point made in the PTA/NEA guide about parents not letting bad personal experiences interfere with the learning opportunities of their children. In our survey study, we found that parents' attitudes about homework often create similar attitudes in their children. Furthermore, at upper grades, positive parent attitudes toward homework were associated with better classroom achievement by their children.

Thus our study demonstrated an important and long-term role for parents' attitudes in shaping their children's attitudes toward homework and influencing the grades of older students. Parents should take these results to mean exactly what the PTA/NEA guide suggests: Don't communicate bad attitudes to children unless you want children to adopt them as well. Teachers and educational policy makers should interpret these results to mean that efforts to improve parent attitudes toward homework are likely to pay off. The lack of a positive effect of homework for some students may be due, in part, to attitudes toward homework held by parents that interfere with, or at least do not support, their children's full participation, persistence, or commitment to completing assignments.

THE OFFICE OF EDUCATIONAL RESEARCH AND IMPROVEMENT (OERI)

The U.S. Department of Education's Office of Educational Research and Improvement has published a guide for parents titled *Helping Your Child With Homework* (Paulu, 1995). The table of contents for the guide summarizes its suggestions for parent involvement in homework:

1. Show you think education and homework are important by setting a regular time, picking a place, removing distractions, providing supplies and identifying resources, setting a good example, showing interest.

2. Monitor assignments by asking about the school's homework policy, being available, looking over completed assignments, monitoring television viewing.

3. Provide guidance by figuring out how your child learns best, helping your child get organized, encouraging good study habits, talking about assignments, giving praise.

4. Talk with someone at school to resolve problems by sharing concerns with teachers and others.

There is little need to reiterate the research that supports most of these suggestions. Paulu's guide for parents certainly embodies the notion that parents should view their role in homework as largely one of providing support and, only secondarily, as playing an active role as teacher.

In sum, both the PTA/NEA and OERI guides provide useful and supportable suggestions for parents regarding their role in homework. In Table 7.1, I provide my own summary of suggestions for parents. And, finally, in Table 7.2, I provide a few tips for parents to share with their children regarding some studying strategy that homework and related research suggest will make the task easier and lead to more learning.

Table 7.1 Homework Tips for Parents

1. Be a stage manager. Make sure your child has a quiet, well-lit place to do homework. Make sure the needed materials (for example, paper, pencils, dictionary) are available.

2. Be a motivator. Homework provides a great opportunity for you to tell your child how important school is. Be positive about homework. The attitude you express about homework will be the attitude your child acquires.

3. Be a role model. When your child does homework, don't sit and watch TV. If your child is reading, you read too. If your child is doing math, balance your checkbook. Help your child see that the skills he or she is practicing are related to things you do as an adult.

4. Be a monitor. Watch your child for signs of failure and frustration. If your child asks for help, provide guidance, not answers. If frustration sets in, suggest a short break.

5. Be a mentor. When the teacher asks that you play a role in homework, do it. If homework is meant to be done alone, stay away. Homework is a great way for kids to develop independent, life-long learning skills. Parental overinvolvement can be a bad thing.

Table 7.2 Homework Tips for Kids

1. Pick a good time to do homework. Try to do your homework at the same time every day—right after school, just before dinner, or right after dinner. Try not to leave homework until just before you go to bed.

2. Remember to make time for long-term projects. Think about using a weekend morning or afternoon for working on big projects, especially if the project involves getting together with classmates. If you need special stuff for a project, make sure to tell your parents to get it for you well in advance.

3. Spend more time on hard homework than easy homework. If you know what's easy and hard, do the hard work first. Take a short break if you are having trouble keeping your mind on an assignment.

4. If homework gets too hard, ask for help. If your parents are busy and you have older brothers or sisters, ask them for help or get your parents to ask them. Ask for help only if you really need it.

5. Find a place that makes studying easy. Collect all the books and supplies you'll need (and your snack) before you begin to work. Do your homework in the same place everyday.

CONCLUSION

In the Preface, I mentioned that I began my studies of homework with no strong disposition about whether it was good or bad. After 15 years of study, my conclusion is, perhaps not surprisingly, that homework can be both good and bad. Homework can be an effective approach to instruction. However, it must serve different purposes at different grade levels. Our expectations for its effects, especially in the short term and in earlier grades, must be modest. It should be one of several approaches we use, along with soccer and the scouts, to show our children that learning takes place everywhere. The question for educators and parents is not which list of effects presented in Chapter 1, the positive or negative, is correct. Any of these effects can happen. To avoid the negative effects, homework policies should give individual schools and teachers some flexibility to take into account the unique needs and circumstances of their students. Teachers should avoid the extremes.

References

Anthony, C. P. (1977). *An experimental study of the effects of different amounts of homework upon student achievement in Algebra I, Algebra II and Algebra III.* Unpublished doctoral dissertation, Rutgers University, New Brunswick, New Jersey.

Bents-Hill, C., Boswell, R., Byers, J., Cohen, N., Cummings, J., & Leavitt, B. (1988, April). *Relationship of academic performance to parent estimate of homework time.* Paper presented at the annual meeting of the National Association of School Psychologists, Chicago, Illinois.

Bradley, R. M. (1967). *An experimental study of individualized versus blanket-type homework assignments in elementary school mathematics.* Unpublished doctoral dissertation, Temple University, Philadelphia, Pennsylvania.

Bryan, T., Burstein, K. M., & Bryan, J. (in press). Factors influencing the homework performance of students with learning disabilities. *Educational Psychologist.*

Comstock, G. (1991). *Television and the American child.* New York: Academic Press.

Cooper, H. (1989). *Homework.* White Plains, NY: Longman.

Cooper, H. (1998). *Synthesizing research: A guide for literature reviews* (3rd ed.). Thousand Oaks, CA: Sage.

Cooper, H., & Hedges, L. V. (1994). *The handbook of research synthesis.* New York: Russell Sage.

Cooper, H., Lindsay, J. J., & Nye, B. (in press). Homework in the home: How student, family and parenting style differences relate to the homework process. *Contemporary Educational Psychology.*

Cooper, H., Lindsay, J. J., Nye, B., & Greathouse, S. (1998). Relationships between attitudes about homework, the amount of homework assigned and completed, and student achievement. *Journal of Educational Psychology, 90,* 70-83.

Cooper, H., & Nye, B. (1994). Homework for students with learning disabilities: Implications of research for policy and practice. *Journal of Learning Disabilities, 27,* 470-479.

Cooper, H., Valentine, J. C., Nye, B., & Lindsay, J. J. (1999). Relationships between five after-school activities and academic achievement. *Journal of Educational Psychology, 91,* 1-10.

Cosden, M., Morrison, G., Albanese, A. L., & Marcias, S. (in press). When homework is not home work: After school programs for homework assistance. *Educational Psychologist.*

Deci, E. L., & Ryan, R. M. (1985). *Intrinsic motivation and self-determination in human behavior.* New York: Plenum.

Epstein, J. L. (1988). *Homework practices, achievements, and behaviors of elementary school students.* Baltimore: Johns Hopkins University, Center for Research on Elementary and Middle Schools.

Epstein, J. L., & Dauber, L. D. (1989). *Effects of the Teachers Involve Parents in Schoolwork (TIPS) social studies and art program on student attitudes and knowledge* (Report No. 41). Baltimore: Johns Hopkins University, Center for Research on Elementary and Middle Schools.

Fredrick, W. C., & Walberg, H. J. (1980). Learning as a function of time. *Journal of Educational Psychology, 73,* 183-194.

Green, P. J., Dugoni, B. L., Ingels, S. J., & Cambrurn, E. (1995). *A profile of the American high school senior in 1992. National Educational Longitudinal Study of 1988: Statistical analysis report.* (ERIC Document Reproduction Service No. ED 386 502)

Grolnick, W. S., & Ryan, R. M. (1989). Parent styles associated with children's self-regulation and competence in school. *Journal of Educational Psychology, 81,* 143-154.

Henderson, M. (1996). *Helping your student get the most out of homework.* Chicago: National Parent Teacher Association and the National Education Association. Retrieved November 2, 2000, from the World Wide Web: www.pta.org/Programs/edulibr/homework.htm

Hinckley, R. H. (Ed.). (1979). *Student home environment, educational achievement and compensatory education.* Santa Monica, CA: Decima Research.

Hudson, J. A. (1965). *A pilot study of the influence of homework in seventh grade mathematics and attitudes toward homework in the Fayetteville public schools.* Unpublished doctoral dissertation, University of Arkansas, Fayetteville.

Keith, T. Z. (1986). *Homework.* West Lafayette, IN: Kappa Delta Pi.

Keith, T. Z., & Cool, V. A. (1992). Testing models of school learning: Effects of quality of instruction, motivation, academic coursework, and homework on academic achievement. *School Psychology Quarterly, 7,* 209-226.

Keith, T. Z., Keith, P. B., Troutman, G. C., Bickley, P. G., Trivette, P. S., & Singh, K. (1993). Does parent involvement affect eighth-grade students achievement? Structural analysis of national data. *School Psychology Review, 22,* 474-496.

Keith, T. Z., Reimers, T. M., Fehrman, P. G., Pottebaum, S. M., & Aubey, P. G. (1986). Parental involvement in homework and TV time: Direct and indirect effects on high school achievement. *Journal of Educational Psychology, 78,* 373-380.

Koch, E. A. (1965). Homework in arithmetic. *The Arithmetic Teacher, 12,* 9-13.

Lipsey, M. W., & Wilson, D. B. (1993). The efficacy of psychological, educational, and behavioral treatment: Confirmation from meta-analysis. *American Psychologist, 48,* 1181-1209.

Marsh, H. W. (1992). Extracurricular activities: Beneficial extension of traditional curriculum or subversion of academic goals? *Journal of Educational Psychology, 84,* 553-562.

Muhlenbruck, L., Cooper, H., Nye, B., & Lindsay, J. J. (2000). Homework and achievement: Explaining the different relations at the elementary and secondary school levels. *Social Psychology of Education, 4,* 295-317.

National Commission on Excellence in Education. (1983). *A nation at risk: The imperative for educational reform.* Washington, DC: U.S. Department of Education.

Otto, H. J. (1950). Elementary education. In *Encyclopedia of educational research* (2nd ed.). New York: Free Press.

Paulu, N. (1995). *Helping your child with homework.* Washington, DC: Office of Educational Research and Improvement.

Roderique, T. W., Polloway, E. A., Cumblad, C., Epstein, M. H., & Bursuck, W. D. (1994). Homework: A survey of policies in the United States. *Journal of Learning Disabilities, 27,* 481-487.

Steinberg, L., Brown, B. B., Cider, M., Kaczmarek, N., & Lazzaro, C. (1988). *Noninstructional influences on adolescent engagement and achievement: The contributions of parents, peers, extracurricular activities, and part-time work.* (ERIC Document Reproduction Service No. ED 307 509)

Tupesis, J. A. (1972). *Mathematics learning as a consequence of the learner's involvement in interaction problem-solving tasks.* Unpublished doctoral dissertation, University of Wisconsin, Madison.

U.S. Department of Education. (1986). *What works.* Washington, DC: Author.

Walberg, H. J. (1986). Synthesis of research on teaching. In M. C. Wittrock (Ed.), *Handbook of research on teaching* (3rd ed., pp. 214-229). New York: Macmillan.

Wildman, P. R. (1968). Homework pressures. *Peabody Journal of Education, 45,* 202-204.

Zill, N., Nord, C. W., & Loomis, L. S. (1995). *Adolescent time use, risky behavior, and outcomes: An analysis of national data.* (ERIC Document Reproduction Service No. ED 386 502)